SCENES

IN THE LIFE OF

HARRIET TUBMAN.

BY

SARAH H. BRADFORD.

AUBURN:
W. J. MOSES, PRINTER.
1869.

STEREOTYPED BY
DENNIS BRO'S & CO.,
AUBURN, N. Y.

HARRIET TUBMAN.

INTRODUCTION.

THE following little story was written by Mrs. Sarah H. Bradford, of Geneva, with the single object of furnishing some help to the subject of the memoir. Harriet Tubman's services and sufferings during the rebellion, which are acknowledged in the letters of Gen. Saxton, and others, it was thought by many, would justify the bestowment of a pension by the Government. But the difficulties in the way of procuring such relief, suggested other methods, and finally the present one. The narrative was prepared on the eve of the author's departure for Europe, where she still remains. It makes no claim whatever to literary merit. Her hope was merely that the considerably numerous public already in part acquainted with Harriet's story, would furnish purchasers enough to secure a little fund for the relief of this remarkable woman. Outside that circle she did not suppose the memoir was likely to meet with much if any sale.

In furtherance of the same benevolent scheme, and in order to secure the whole avails of the work for Harriet's benefit, a subscription has been raised more than sufficient to defray the entire cost of publication. This has been effected by the generous exertions of Wm. G. Wise, Esq., of this city. The whole amount was contributed by citizens of Auburn, with the exception of two liberal subscriptions by Gerrit Smith, Esq., and Mr. Wendell Phillips.

Mr. Wise has also consented, at Mrs. Bradford's request, to act as trustee for Harriet; and will receive, invest, and apply, for her benefit, whatever may accrue from the sale of this book.

The spirited wood-cut likeness of Harriet, in her costume as scout, was furnished by the kindness of Mr. J. C. Darby, of this city. S. M. H.

AUBURN, Dec. 1, 1868.

PREFACE.

It is proposed in this little book to give a plain and unvarnished account of some scenes and adventures in the life of a woman who, though one of earth's lowly ones, and of dark-hued skin, has shown an amount of heroism in her character rarely possessed by those of any station in life. Her name (we say it advisedly and without exaggeration) deserves to be handed down to posterity side by side with the names of Joan of Arc, Grace Darling, and Florence Nightingale; for not one of these women has shown more courage and power of endurance in facing danger and death to relieve human suffering, than has this woman in her heroic and successful endeavors to reach and save all whom she might of her oppressed and suffering race, and to pilot them from the land of Bondage to the promised land of Liberty. Well has she been called "*Moses*," for she has been a leader and deliverer unto hundreds of her people.

Worn down by her sufferings and fatigues, her health permanently affected by the cruelties to which she has been subjected, she is still laboring to the utmost limit of her strength for the support of her aged parents, and still also for her afflicted people—by her own efforts supporting two schools for Freedmen at the South, and supplying them with clothes and books; never obtruding herself, never asking for charity, except for "her people."

It is for the purpose of aiding her in ministering to the wants of her aged parents, and in the hope of securing to them the little home which they are in danger of losing from inability to pay the whole amount due—which amount was partly paid when our heroine left them to throw herself into the work of aiding our suffering soldiers—that this little account, drawn from her by persevering endeavor, is given to the friends of humanity.

The writer of this story has till very lately known less personally of the subject of it, than many others to whom she has for years been an object of interest and care. But through relations and friends in Auburn, and also through Mrs. Commodore Swift of Geneva, and her sisters, who have for many years known and esteemed this wonderful woman, she has heard tales of her deeds of heroism which seemed almost too strange for belief, and were invested with the charm of romance.

During a sojourn of some months in the city of Auburn, while the war was in progress, the writer used to see occasionally in her Sunday-school class the aged mother of Harriet, and also some of those girls who had been brought from the South by this remarkable woman. She also wrote letters for the old people to commanding officers at the South, making inquiries about Harriet, and received answers telling of her untiring devotion to our wounded and sick soldiers, and of her efficient aid in various ways to the cause of the Union.

By the graphic pen of Mrs. Stowe, the incidents of such a life as that of the subject of this little memoir might be wrought up into a tale of thrilling interest, equaling, if not exceeding, anything in her world-renowned "Uncle Tom's Cabin;" but the story of Harriet Tubman needs not the drapery of fiction; the bare unadorned facts are enough to stir the hearts of the friends of humanity, the friends of liberty, the lovers of their country.

There are those who will sneer, there are those who have already done so, at this *quixotic attempt* to make a heroine of a black woman, and a slave; but it may possibly be that there are some natures, though concealed under fairer skins, who have not the capacity to comprehend such general and self-sacrificing devotion to the cause of others as that here delineated, and therefore they resort to scorn and ridicule, in order to throw discredit upon the whole story.

Much has been left out which would have been highly interesting, because of the impossibility of substantiating by the testimony of others the truth of Harriet's statements. But whenever it has been possible to find those who were cognizant with the facts stated, they have been corroborated in every particular.

A few years hence and we seem to see a gathering where the wrongs of earth will be righted, and Justice, long delayed, will assert itself, and perform its office. Then not a few of those who had esteemed themselves the wise and noble of this world, "will begin with shame to take the lowest place;" while upon Harriet's dark head a kind hand will be placed, and in her ear a gentle voice will sound, saying: "Friend! come up higher!"

S. H. B.

The following letters to the writer from those well-known and distinguished philanthropists, Hon.

Gerrit Smith and Wendell Phillips, and one from Frederick Douglass, addressed to Harriet, will serve as the best introduction that can be given of the subject of this memoir to its readers:

Letter from Hon. Gerrit Smith.

PETERBORO, June 13, 1868.

MY DEAR MADAME: I am happy to learn that you are to speak to the public of Mrs. Harriet Tubman. Of the remarkable events of her life I have no *personal* knowledge, but of the truth of them as she describes them I have no doubt.

I have often listened to her, in her visits to my family, and I am confident that she is not only truthful, but that she has a rare discernment, and a deep and sublime philanthropy.

With great respect your friend,

GERRIT SMITH.

Letter from Wendell Phillips.

JUNE 16, 1868.

DEAR MADAME: The last time I ever saw John Brown was under my own roof, as he brought Harriet Tubman to me, saying: "Mr. Phillips, I bring you one of the best and bravest persons on this continent—*General* Tubman, as we call her."

He then went on to recount her labors and sacrifices in behalf of her race. After that, Harriet spent some time in Boston, earning the confidence and admiration of all those who were working for freedom. With their aid she went to the South more than once, returning always with a squad of self-emancipated men, women, and children, for whom her marvelous skill had opened the way of escape. After the war broke out, she was sent with indorsements from Governor Andrew and his friends to South Carolina, where in the service of the Nation she rendered most important and efficient aid to our army.

In my opinion there are few captains, perhaps few colonels, who have done more for the loyal cause since the war began, and few men who did before that time more for the colored race, than our fearless and most sagacious friend, Harriet.

Faithfully yours,

WENDELL PHILLIPS.

Letter from Frederick Douglass.

ROCHESTER, August 29, 1868.

DEAR HARRIET: I am glad to know that the story of your eventful life has been written by a kind lady, and that the same is soon to be published. You ask for what you do not need when you call upon me for a word of commendation. I need such words from you far more than you can need them from me, especially where your superior labors and devotion to the cause of the lately enslaved of our land are known as I know them. The difference between us is very marked. Most that I have done and suffered in the service of our cause has been in public, and I have received much encouragement at every step of the way. You on the other hand have labored in a private way. I have wrought in the day—you in the night. I have had the applause of the crowd and the satisfaction that comes of being approved by the multitude, while the most that you have done has been witnessed by a few trembling, scarred, and foot-sore bondmen and women, whom you have led out of the house of bondage, and whose heartfelt "*God bless you*" has been your only reward. The midnight sky and the silent stars have been the witnesses of your devotion to freedom and of your heroism. Excepting John Brown—of sacred memory—I know of no one who has willingly encountered more perils and hardships to serve our enslaved people than you have. Much that you have done would seem improbable to those who do not know you as I know you. It is to me a great pleasure and a great privilege to bear testimony to your character and your works, and to say to those to whom you may come, that I regard you in every way truthful and trustworthy.

Your friend,

FREDERICK DOUGLASS.

SOME SCENES

IN THE

LIFE OF HARRIET TUBMAN.

HARRIET TUBMAN, known at various times, and in various places, by many different names, such as "Moses," in allusion to her being the leader and guide to so many of her people in their exodus from the Land of Bondage; "the Conductor of the Underground Railroad;" and "Moll Pitcher," for the energy and daring by which she delivered a fugitive slave who was about to be dragged back to the South; was for the first twenty-five years of her life a slave on the eastern shore of Maryland. Her own master she represents as never unnecessarily cruel; but as was common among slaveholders, he often hired out his slaves to others, some of whom proved to be tyrannical and brutal to the utmost limit of their power.

She had worked only as a field-hand for many years, following the oxen, loading and unloading wood, and carrying heavy burdens, by which her naturally remarkable power of muscle was so developed that her feats of strength often called forth the wonder of strong laboring men. Thus was she preparing for the life of hardship and endurance which lay before her, for the deeds of daring she was to do, and of which her ignorant and darkened mind at that time never dreamed.

The first person by whom she was hired was a woman who, though married and the mother of a family, was still "Miss Susan" to her slaves, as is customary at the South. This woman was possessed of the good things of this life, and provided liberally for her slaves—so far as food and clothing went. But she had been brought up to believe, and to act upon the belief, that a slave could be taught to do nothing, and *would* do nothing but under the sting of the whip. Harriet, then a young girl, was taken from her life in the field, and having never seen the inside of a house better than a cabin in the negro quarters, was put to house-work without being told how to do anything. The first thing was to put a parlor in order. "Move these chairs and tables into the middle of the room, sweep the carpet clean, then dust everything, and put them back in their places!" These were the directions given, and Harriet was left alone to do her work.

The whip was in sight on the mantel-piece, as a reminder of what was to be expected if the work was not done well. Harriet fixed the furniture as she was told to do, and swept with all her strength, raising a tremendous dust. The moment she had finished sweeping, she took her dusting cloth, and wiped everything "so you could see your face in 'em, de shone so," in haste to go and set the table for breakfast, and do her other work. The dust which she had set flying only settled down again on chairs, tables, and the piano. "Miss Susan" came in and looked around. Then came the call for "Minty"—Harriet's name was Araminta at the South.

She drew her up to the table, saying, "What do you mean by doing my work this way, you—!" and passing her finger on the table and piano, she showed her the mark it made through the dust. "Miss Susan, I done sweep and dust jus' as you tole me." But the whip was already taken down, and the strokes were falling on head and face and neck. Four times this scene was repeated before breakfast, when, during the fifth whipping, the door opened, and "Miss Emily" came in. She was a married sister of "Miss Susan," and was making her a visit, and though brought up with the same associations as her sister, seems to have been a person of more gentle and reasonable nature. Not being able to endure the screams of the child any longer, she came in, took her sister by the arm, and said, "If you do not stop whipping that child, I will leave your house, and never come back!" Miss Susan declared that "she *would* not mind, and she slighted her work on purpose." Miss Emily said, "Leave her to me a few moments;" and Miss Susan left the room, indignant. As soon as they were alone, Miss Emily said: "Now, Minty, show me how you do your work." For the sixth time Harriet removed all the furniture into the middle of the room; then she swept; and the moment she had done sweeping, she took the dusting cloth to wipe off the furniture. "Now stop there," said Miss Emily; "go away now, and do some of your other work, and when it is time to dust, I will call you." When the time came she called her, and explained to her how the dust had now settled, and that if she wiped it off now, the furniture would remain bright and clean. These few words an hour or two before, would have saved Harriet her whippings for that day, as they probably did for many a day after.

While with this woman, after working from early

morning till late at night, she was obliged to sit up all night to rock a cross, sick child. Her mistress laid upon her bed with a whip under her pillow, and slept; but if the tired nurse forgot herself for a moment, if her weary head dropped, and her hand ceased to rock the cradle, the child would cry out, and then down would come the whip upon the neck and face of the poor weary creature. The scars are still plainly visible where the whip cut into the flesh. Perhaps her mistress was preparing her, though she did not know it then, by this enforced habit of wakefulness, for the many long nights of travel, when she was the leader and guide of the weary and hunted ones who were escaping from bondage.

"Miss Susan" got tired of Harriet, as Harriet was determined she should do, and so abandoned her intention of buying her, and sent her back to her master. She was next hired out to the man who inflicted upon her the life-long injury from which she is suffering now, by breaking her skull with a weight from the scales. The injury thus inflicted causes her often to fall into a state of somnolency from which it is almost impossible to rouse her. Disabled and sick, her flesh all wasted away, she was returned to her *owner*. He tried to sell her, but no one would buy her. "Dey said dey wouldn't give a sixpence for me," she said.

"And so," she said, "from Christmas till March I worked as I could, and I *prayed* through all the long nights—I groaned and prayed for ole master: 'Oh Lord, convert master!' 'Oh Lord, change dat man's heart!' 'Pears like I prayed all de time," said Harriet; "'bout my work, everywhere, I prayed an' I groaned to de Lord. When I went to de horse-trough to wash my face, I took up de water in my han' an' I said, 'Oh Lord, wash me, make me clean!' Den I take up something to wipe my face, an' I say, 'Oh Lord, wipe away all my sin!' When I took de broom and began to sweep, I groaned, 'Oh Lord, wha'soebber sin dere be in my heart, sweep it out, Lord, clar an' clean!'" No words can describe the pathos of her tones, as she broke out into these words of prayer, after the manner of her people. "An' so," said she, "I prayed all night long for master, till the first of March; an' all the time he was bringing people to look at me, an' trying to sell me. Den we heard dat some of us was gwine to be sole to go wid de chain-gang down to de cotton an' rice fields, and dey said I was gwine, an' my brudders, an' sisters. Den I changed my prayer. Fust of March

I began to pray, 'Oh Lord, if you ant nebber gwine to change dat man's heart, kill him, Lord, an' take him out ob de way.'

"Nex' ting I heard old master was dead, an' he died jus' as he libed. Oh, then, it 'peared like I'd give all de world full ob gold, if I had it, to bring dat poor soul back. But I couldn't pray for him no longer."

The slaves were told that their master's will provided that none of them should be sold out of the State. This satisfied most of them, and they were very happy. But Harriet was not satisfied; she never closed her eyes that she did not imagine she saw the horsemen coming, and heard the screams of women and children, as they were being dragged away to a far worse slavery than that they were enduring there. Harriet was married at this time to a free negro, who not only did not trouble himself about her fears, but did his best to betray her, and bring her back after she escaped. She would start up at night with the cry, "Oh, dey're comin', dey're comin', I mus' go!"

Her husband called her a fool, and said she was like old Cudjo, who when a joke went round, never laughed till half an hour after everybody else got through, and so just as all danger was past she began to be frightened. But still Harriet in fancy saw the horsemen coming, and heard the screams of terrified women and children. "And all that time, in my dreams and visions," she said, "I seemed to see a line, and on the other side of that line were green fields, and lovely flowers, and beautiful white ladies, who stretched out their arms to me over the line, but I couldn't reach them nohow. I always fell before I got to the line."

One Saturday it was whispered in the quarters that two of Harriet's sisters had been sent off with the chain-gang. That morning she started, having persuaded three of her brothers to accompany her, but they had not gone far when the brothers, appalled by the dangers before and behind them, determined to go back, and in spite of her remonstrances dragged her with them. In fear and terror, she remained over Sunday, and on Monday night a negro from another part of the plantation came privately to tell Harriet that herself and brothers were to be carried off that night. The poor old mother, who belonged to the same mistress, was just going to milk. Harriet wanted to get away without letting her know, because she knew that she would raise an uproar and prevent her going, or insist upon going with her, and the time for this was not yet. But she must give some intimation to those she was going to leave of her intention, and send such a farewell as she might to the friends and relations on the plantation. These communications were generally made by singing. They sang as they walked along the country roads, and the chorus was taken up by others, and the uninitiated knew not the hidden meaning of the words—

When dat ar ole chariot comes,
  I'm gwine to lebe you;
I'm boun' for de promised land,
  I'm gwine to lebe you.

These words meant something more than a journey to the Heavenly Canaan. Harriet said, "Here, mother, go 'long; I'll do the milkin' to-night and bring it in." The old woman went to her cabin. Harriet took down her sun-bonnet, and went on to the "big house," where some of her relatives lived as house servants. She thought she could trust Mary, but there were others in the kitchen, and she could say nothing. Mary began to frolic with her. She threw her across the kitchen, and ran out, knowing that Mary would follow her. But just as they turned the corner of the house, the master to whom Harriet was now hired, came riding up on his horse. Mary darted back, and Harriet thought there was no way now but to sing. But "the Doctor," as the master was called, was regarded with special awe by his slaves; if they were singing or talking together in the field, or on the road, and "the Doctor" appeared, all was hushed till he passed. But Harriet had no time for ceremony; her friends must have a warning; and whether the Doctor thought her "*imperent*" or not, she must sing him farewell. So on she went to meet him, singing:

> I'm sorry I'm gwine to lebe you,
> Farewell, oh farewell;
> But I'll meet you in the mornin',
> Farewell, oh farewell.

The Doctor passed, and she bowed as she went on, still singing:

> I'll meet you in the mornin',
> I'm boun' for de promised land,
> On the oder side of Jordan,
> Boun' for de promised land.

She reached the gate and looked round; the Doctor had stopped his horse, and had turned around in the saddle, and was looking at her as if there might be more in this than "met the ear." Harriet closed the gate, went on a little way, came back, the Doctor still gazing at her. She lifted up the gate as if she had not latched it properly, waved her hand to him, and burst out again:

I'll meet you in the mornin',
Safe in de promised land,
On the oder side of Jordan,
Boun' for de promised land.

And she started on her journey, "not knowing whither she went," except that she was going to follow the north star, till it led her to liberty. Cautiously and by night she traveled, cunningly feeling her way, and finding out who were friends; till after a long and painful journey she found, in answer to careful inquiries, that she had at last crossed that magic "line" which then separated the land of bondage from the land of freedom; for this was before *we* were commanded by law to take part in the iniquity of slavery, and aid in taking and sending back those poor hunted fugitives who had manhood and intelligence enough to enable them to make their way thus far towards freedom.

"When I found I had crossed dat *line*," she said, "I looked at my hands to see if I was de same pusson. There was such a glory ober ebery ting; de sun came like gold through the trees, and ober the fields, and I felt like I was in Heaben."

But then came the bitter drop in the cup of joy. She said she felt like a man who was put in State Prison for twenty-five years. All these twenty-five years he was thinking of his home, and longing for the time when he would see it again. At last the day comes—he leaves the prison gates—he makes his way to his old home, but his old home is not there. The house has been pulled down, and a new one has been put up in its place; his family and friends are gone nobody knows where; there is no one to take him by the hand, no one to welcome him.

"So it was with me," she said. "I had crossed the line. I was *free;* but there was no one to welcome me to the land of freedom. I was a stranger in a strange land; and my home, after all, was down in Maryland; because my father, my mother, my brothers, and sisters, and friends were there. But I was free, and *they* should be free. I would make a home in the North and bring them there, God helping me. Oh, how I prayed then," she said; "I said to de Lord, 'I'm gwine to hole stiddy on to *you*, an' I *know* you'll see me through.'"

She came to Philadelphia, and worked in hotels, in club houses, and afterwards at Cape May. Whenever she had raised money enough to pay expenses, she would make her way back, hide herself, and in various ways give notice to those who were ready to strike for freedom. When her party was made up, they would start always on Saturday night, because advertisements could not be sent out on Sunday, which gave them one day in advance.

Then the pursuers would start after them. Advertisements would be posted everywhere. There was one reward of $12,000 offered for the head of the woman who was constantly appearing and enticing away parties of slaves from their master. She had traveled in the cars when these posters were put up over her head, and she heard them read by those about her—for she could not read herself. Fearlessly she went on, trusting in the Lord. She said, "I started with this idea in my head, 'Dere's *two* things I've got a *right* to, and dese are, Death or Liberty—one or tother I mean to have. No one will take me back alive; I shall fight for my liberty, and when de time has come for me to go, de Lord will let dem kill me." And acting upon this simple creed, and firm in this trusting faith, she went back and forth *nineteen times*, according to the reckoning of her friends. She remembers that she went eleven times from Canada, but of the other journeys she kept no reckoning.

While Harriet was working as cook in one of

the large hotels in Philadelphia, the play of "Uncle Tom's Cabin" was being performed for many weeks every night. Some of her fellow-servants wanted her to go and see it. "No," said Harriet, "I haint got no heart to go and see the sufferings of my people played on de stage. I've heard 'Uncle Tom's Cabin' read, and I tell you Mrs Stowe's pen hasn't begun to paint what slavery is as I have seen it at the far South. I've seen de *real ting*, and I don't want to see it on no stage or in no teater."

I will give here an article from a paper published nearly a year ago, which mentions that the price set upon the head of Harriet was much higher than I have stated it to be. When asked about this, Harriet said she did not know whether it was so, but she heard them read from one paper that the reward offered was $12,000.

"Among American women," says the article referred to, "who has shown a courage and self-devotion to the welfare of others, equal to Harriet Tubman? Hear her story of going down again and again into the very jaws of slavery, to rescue her suffering people, bringing them off through perils and dangers enough to appall the stoutest heart, till she was known among them as 'Moses.'

"*Forty thousand dollars* was not too great a

reward for the Maryland slaveholders to offer for her.

"Think of her brave spirit, as strong as Daniel's of old, in its fearless purpose to serve God, even though the fiery furnace should be her portion. I have looked into her dark face, and wondered and admired as I listened to the thrilling deeds her lion heart had prompted her to dare. 'I have heard their groans and sighs, and seen their tears, and I would give every drop of blood in my veins to free them,' she said.

"The other day, at Gerrit Smith's, I saw this heroic woman, whom the pen of genius will yet make famous, as one of the noblest Christian hearts ever inspired to lift the burdens of the wronged and oppressed, and what do you think she said to me? She had been tending and caring for our Union black (and white) soldiers in hospital during the war, and at the end of her labors was on her way home, coming in a car through New Jersey. A white man, the conductor, thrust her out of the car with such violence that she has not been able to work scarcely any since; and as she told me of the pain she had and still suffered, she said she did not know what she should have done for herself, and the old father and mother she takes care of, if Mr. Wendell

Phillips had not sent her $60, that kept them warm through the winter. She had a letter from W. H. Seward to Maj.-Gen. Hunter, in which he says, 'I have known her long, and a nobler, higher spirit, or truer, seldom dwells in the human form.'"

It will be impossible to give any connected account of the different journeys taken by Harriet for the rescue of her people, as she herself has no idea of the dates connected with them, or of the order in which they were made. She thinks she was about 25 when she made her own escape, and this was in the last year of James K. Polk's administration. From that time till the beginning of the war, her years were spent in these journeyings back and forth, with intervals between, in which she worked only to spend the avails of her labor in providing for the wants of her next party of fugitives. By night she traveled, many times on foot, over mountains, through forests, across rivers, mid perils by land, perils by water, perils from enemies, "perils among false brethren." Sometimes members of her party would become exhausted, foot-sore, and bleeding, and declare they could not go on, they must stay where they dropped down, and die; others would think a voluntary return to slavery better than being overtaken and carried back, and would insist upon returning; then there was no remedy but force; the revolver carried by this bold and daring pioneer would be pointed at their heads. "Dead niggers tell no tales," said Harriet; "Go on or die;" and so she compelled them to drag their weary limbs on their northward journey.

At one time she collected and sent on a gang of thirty-nine fugitives in the care of others, as from some cause she was prevented from accompanying them. Sometimes, when she and her party were concealed in the woods, they saw their pursuers pass, on their horses, down the high road, tacking up the advertisements for them on the fences and trees.

"And den how we laughed," said she. "*We* was de fools, and *dey* was de wise men; but we wasn't fools enough to go down de high road in de broad daylight." At one time she left her party in the woods, and went by a long and roundabout way to one of the "stations of the Underground Railway," as she called them. Here she procured food for her famished party, often paying out of her hardly-gained earnings, five dollars a day for food for them. But she dared not go back to them till night, for fear of being watched, and thus revealing their hiding-place. After nightfall, the sound of a hymn sung at a distance comes upon the ears of the concealed and famished fugitives in the woods, and they know that their deliverer is at hand. They listen eagerly for the words she sings, for by them they are to be warned of danger, or informed of safety. Nearer and nearer comes the unseen singer, and the words are wafted to their ears:

Hail, oh hail ye happy spirits,
  Death no more shall make you fear,
No grief nor sorrow, pain nor anger (anguish)
  Shall no more distress you there.

Around him are ten thousan' angels,
  Always ready to 'bey comman'.
Dey are always hobring round you,
  Till you reach the hebbenly lan'.

Jesus, Jesus will go wid you;
  He will lead you to his throne;
He who died has gone before you,
  Trod de wine-press all alone.

He whose thunders shake creation;
  He who bids the planets roll;
He who rides upon the temple, (tempest)
  An' his scepter sways de whole.

Dark and thorny is de desert,
  Through de pilgrim makes his ways,
Yet beyon' dis vale of sorrow,
  Lies de fiel's of endless days.

I give these words exactly as Harriet sang them to me to a sweet and simple Methodist air. "De first time I go by singing dis hymn, dey don't come out to me," she said, "till I listen if de coast is clar; den when I go back and sing it again, dey come out. But if I sing:

Moses go down in Egypt,
  Till ole Pharo' let me go;
Hadn't been for Adam's fall,
  Shouldn't hab to died at all,

den dey don't come out, for dere's danger in de way."

And so by night travel, by hiding, by signals, by threatening, she brought the people safely to the land of liberty. But after the passage of the Fugitive Slave law, she said, "I wouldn't trust Uncle Sam wid my people no longer; I brought 'em all clar off to Canada."

Of the very many interesting stories told me by Harriet, I cannot refrain from telling to my readers that of *Joe*, who accompanied her upon her seventh or eighth journey from Maryland to Canada.

Joe was a noble specimen of a negro, and was hired out by his master to a man for whom he worked faithfully for six years, saving him the expense of an overseer, and taking all trouble off his hands. At length this man found him so absolutely necessary to him, that he determined to buy him at any cost. His master held him proportionably high. However, by paying a thousand dollars down for him, and promising to pay another thousand in a certain time, Joe passed into the hands of his new master.

As may be imagined, Joe was somewhat surprised when the first order issued from his master's lips, was, "Now, Joe, strip and take a whipping!" Joe's experience of *whippings*, as he had seen them inflicted upon others, was not such as to cause him particularly to desire to go through the same operation on his own account; and he, naturally enough, demurred, and at first thought of resisting. But he called to mind a scene which he had witnessed a few days before, in the field, the particulars of which are too horrible and too harassing to the feelings to be given to my readers, and he thought it best to submit; but first he tried remonstrance.

"Mas'r," said he, "habn't I always been faithful to you? Habn't I worked through sun an' rain, early in de mornin', and late at night; habn't I saved you an oberseer by doin' his work; hab you anyting to complain of agin me?"

"No, Joe; "I've no complaint to make of you; you're a good nigger, and you've always worked well; but the first lesson my niggers have to learn is that I am *master*, and that they are not to resist or refuse to obey anything I tell 'em to do. So the first thing they've got to do, is to be whipped; if they resist, they get it all the harder; and so I'll go on, till I kill 'em, but they've got to give up at last, and learn that I'm master."

Joe thought it best to submit. He stripped off his upper clothing, and took his whipping without a word; but as he drew his clothes up over his torn and bleeding back, he said, "Dis is de last!" That night he took a boat and went a long distance to the cabin of Harriet's father, and said, "Next time Moses comes, let me know." It was only a week or two after that, that the mysterious woman whom no one could lay their finger on appeared, and men, women, and children began to disappear from the plantations. One fine morning Joe was missing, and his brother William, from another plantation; Peter and Eliza, too, were gone; and these made part of Harriet's next party, who began their pilgrimage from Maryland to Canada, or as they expressed it, from "Egypt to de land of Canaan."

Their adventures were enough to fill a volume; they were pursued; they were hidden in "potato holes," while their pursuers passed within a few feet of them; they were passed along by friends in various disguises; they scattered and separated, to be led by guides by a roundabout way, to a meeting-place again. They were taken in by Sam Green, the man who was afterwards sent to State Prison for ten years for having a copy of "Uncle Tom's Cabin" in his house; and so, hunted and hiding and wandering, they came at last to the long bridge at the entrance of the city of Wilmington, Delaware. The rewards posted up everywhere had been at first five hundred dollars for Joe, if taken within the limits of the United States; then a thousand, and then fifteen hundred dollars, "an' all expenses clar an' clean, for his body in Easton Jail." Eight hundred for William, and four hundred for Peter, and twelve thousand for the woman who enticed them away. The long Wilmington Bridge was guarded by police officers, and the advertisements were everywhere. The party were scattered, and taken to the houses of different colored friends, and word was sent secretly to Thomas Garrett, of Wilmington, of their condition, and the necessity of their being taken across the bridge. Thomas Garrett is a Quaker, and a man of a wonderfully large and generous heart, through whose hands, Harriet tells me, two thousand self-emancipated slaves passed on their way to freedom. He was always ready, heart and hand and means, in aiding these poor fugitives, and rendered most efficient help to Harriet on many of her journeys back and forth. A letter received a few days since by the writer, from this noble-hearted philanthropist, will be given presently.

As soon as Thomas Garrett heard of the condition of these poor people, his plan was formed. He engaged two wagons, filled them with bricklayers, whom of course he paid well for their share in the enterprise, and sent them across the bridge. They went as if on a frolic, singing and shouting. The guards saw them pass, and of course expected them to re-cross the bridge. After nightfall (and fortunately it was a dark night) the same wagons went back, but with an addition to their party. The fugitives were on the bottom of the wagons, the bricklayers on the seats, still singing and shouting; and so they passed by the guards, who were entirely unsuspicious of the nature of the load the wagons contained, or of the amount of property thus escaping their hands. And so they made their way to New York. When they entered the anti-slavery office there, Joe was recognized at once by the description in the advertisement. "Well," said Mr. Oliver Johnson, "I am glad to see the man whose head is worth fifteen hundred dollars." At this Joe's heart sank. If the advertisement had got to New York, that place which it had taken them so many days and nights to reach, he thought he was in danger still. "And how far is it now to Canada?" he asked. When told how many miles, for they were to come through New York State, and cross the Suspension Bridge, he was ready to give up. "From dat time Joe was silent," said Harriet; "he sang no more, he talked no more; he sat wid his head on his hand, and nobody could 'muse him or make him take any interest in anyting." They passed along in safety, and at length found themselves in the cars, approaching Suspension Bridge. The rest were very joyous and happy, but Joe sat silent and sad. Their fellow-passengers all seemed interested in and for them, and listened with tears, as Harriet and all their party lifted up their voices and sang:

I'm on my way to Canada,
  That cold and dreary land;
The sad effects of slavery,
  I can't no longer stand.
I've served my master all my days,
  Widout a dime's reward;
And now I'm forced to run away,
  To flee the lash abroad.
Farewell, ole master, don't think hard of me,
I'll travel on to Canada, where all the slaves are free.

The hounds are baying on my track,
Ole master comes behind.
Resolved that he will bring me back,
Before I cross de line;
I'm now embarked for yonder shore,
There a man's a man by law;
The iron horse will bear me o'er,
To shake de lion's paw.
Oh, righteous Father, wilt thou not pity me,
And aid me on to Canada where all the slaves are free.

Oh, I heard Queen Victoria say,
That if we would forsake
Our native land of slavery,
And come across the lake;
That she was standin' on de shore,
Wid arms extended wide,
To give us all a peaceful home
Beyond de rolling tide.
Farewell, ole master, etc.

The cars began to cross the bridge. Harriet was very anxious to have her companions see the Falls. William, Peter, and Eliza came eagerly to look at the wonderful sight; but Joe sat still, with his head upon his hand.

"Joe, come look at de Falls! Joe, you fool you, come see de Falls! its your last chance." But Joe sat still and never raised his head. At length Harriet knew by the rise in the center of the bridge, and the descent on the other side, that they had crossed "the line." She sprang across to Joe's seat, shook him with all her might, and shouted, "Joe, you've shook de lion's paw!" Joe did not know what she meant. "Joe, you're *free!*" shouted Harriet. Then Joe's head went up, he raised his hands on high, and his face, streaming with tears, to heaven, and broke out in loud and thrilling tones:

> "Glory to God and Jesus too,
> One more soul is safe!
> Oh, go and carry de news,
> One more soul got safe."

"Joe, come and look at de Falls!" called Harriet.

> "Glory to God and Jesus too,
> One more soul got safe."

was all the answer. The cars stopped on the other side. Joe's feet were the first to touch British soil, after those of the conductor.

Loud roared the waters of Niagara, but louder still ascended the anthem of praise from the overflowing heart of the freeman. And can we doubt that the strain was taken up by angel voices, and that through the arches of Heaven echoed and reechoed the strain:

> Glory to God in the Highest,
> Glory to God and Jesus too,
> One more soul is safe.

"The ladies and gentlemen gathered round him," said Harriet, "till I couldn't see Joe for the crowd, only I heard 'Glory to God and Jesus too!' louder than ever." William went after him, and pulled him, saying, "Joe, stop your noise! you act like a fool!' Then Peter ran in and jerked him mos' off his feet,—"Joe, stop your hollerin'! Folks 'll think you're crazy!" But Joe gave no heed. The ladies were crying, and the tears like rain ran down Joe's sable cheeks. A lady reached over her fine cambric handkerchief to him. Joe wiped his face, and then he spoke.

"Oh! if I'd felt like dis down South, it would hab taken *nine* men to take me; only one more journey for me now, and dat is to Hebben!" "Well, you ole fool you," said Harriet, with whom there seems but one step from the sublime to the ridiculous, "you might a' looked at de Falls fust, and den gone to Hebben afterwards." She has seen Joe several times since, a happy and industrious freeman in Canada.

When asked, as she often is, how it was possible that she was not afraid to go back, with that tremendous price upon her head, Harriet always answers, "Why, don't I tell you, Missus, t'wan't *me*, 'twas *de Lord!* I always *tole* him, 'I trust to you. I don't know where to go or what to do, but I expect you to lead me,' an' he always did." At one time she was going down, watched for everywhere, after there had been a meeting of slaveholders in the court-house of one of the large cities of Maryland, and an added reward had been put upon her head, with various threats of the different cruel devices by which she should be tortured and put to death; friends gathered round her, imploring her not to go on directly in the face of danger and death, and this was Harriet's answer to them:

"Now look yer! John saw the city, didn't he? Yes, John saw the city. Well, what did he see? He saw twelve gates—three of dose gates was on de north—three of 'em was on de east—and three of 'em was on de west—but dere was three of 'em on de *South* too; an' I reckon if dey kill me down dere, I'll git into one of dem gates, don't you?"

Whether Harriet's ideas of the geographical bearings of the gates of the Celestial City, as seen in the Apocalyptic vision, were correct or not, we cannot doubt that she was right in the deduction her faith drew from them; and that *somewhere*, whether north, south, east, or west, to our dim vision, there is a gate to be opened for Harriet, where the welcome will be given, "Come in thou blessed of my Father."

Many of the stories told me by Harriet, in answer to questions, have been corroborated by letters, some of which will appear in this book. Of others, I have not been able to procure confirmation, owing to ignorance of the address of those conversant with the facts. I find among her papers, many of which are defaced by being carried about with her for years, portions of letters addressed to myself, by persons at the South, and speaking of the valuable assistance Harriet was rendering our soldiers in the hospital, and our armies in the field. At this time her manner of life, as related by herself, was this:

"Well, Missus, I'd go to de hospital, I would, early eb'ry mornin'. I'd get a big chunk of ice, I would, and put it in a basin, and fill it with water; den I'd take a sponge and begin. Fust man I'd come to, I'd thrash away de flies, an' dey'd rise, dey would, like bees roun' a hive. Den I'd begin to bathe der wounds, an' by de time I'd bathed off three or four, de fire and heat would have melted de ice and made de water warm, an' it would be as red as clar blood. Den I'd go an' git more ice, I would, an' by de time I got to de nex' ones, de flies would be roun' de fust ones black an' thick as eber." In this way she worked, day after day, till late at night; then she went home to her little cabin, and made about fifty pies, a great quantity of ginger-bread, and two casks of root beer. These she would hire some contraband to sell for her through the camps, and thus she would provide her support for another day; for this woman never received pay or pension, and never drew for herself but twenty days' rations during the four years of her labors. At one time she was called away from Hilton Head, by one of our officers, to come to Fernandina, where the men were "dying off like sheep," from dysentery. Harriet had acquired quite a reputation for her skill in curing this disease, by a medicine which she prepared from roots which grew near the waters which gave the disease. Here she found thousands of sick soldiers and contrabands, and immediately gave up her time and attention to them. At another time, we find her nursing those who were down by hundreds with small-pox and malignant fevers. She had never had these diseases, but she seems to have no more fear of death in one form than another. "De Lord would take keer of her till her time came, an' den she was ready to go."

When our armies and gun-boats first appeared in any part of the South, many of the poor negroes were as much afraid of "de Yankee Buckra" as of their own masters. It was almost impossible to win their confidence, or to get information from them. But to Harriet they would tell anything; and so it became quite important that she should accompany expeditions going up the rivers, or into unexplored parts of the country, to control and get information from those whom they took with them as guides.

Gen. Hunter asked her at one time if she would go with several gun-boats up the Combahee River, the object of the expedition being to take up the torpedoes placed by the rebels in the river, to destroy railroads and bridges, and to cut off supplies from the rebel troops. She said she would go if Col. Montgomery was to be appointed commander of the expedition. Col. Montgomery was one of John Brown's men, and was well known to Harriet. Accordingly, Col. Montgomery was appointed to the command, and Harriet, with several men under her, the principal of whom was J. Plowden, whose pass I have, accompanied the expedition. Harriet describes in the most graphic manner the appearance of the plantations as they passed up the river; the frightened negroes leaving their work and taking to the woods, at sight of the gun-boats; then coming to peer out like startled deer, and scudding away like the wind at the sound of the steam-whistle. "Well," said one old negro, "Mas'r said de Yankees had horns and tails, but I nebber beliebed it till now." But the word was passed along by the mysterious telegraphic communication existing among these simple people, that these were "Lincoln's gun-boats come to set them free." In vain, then, the drivers used their whips, in their efforts to hurry the poor creatures back to their quarters; they all turned and ran for the gun-boats. They came down every road, across every field, just as they had left their work and their cabins; women with children clinging around their necks, hanging to their dresses, running behind, all making at full speed for "Lincoln's gun-boats." Eight hundred poor wretches at one time crowded the banks, with their hands extended towards their deliverers, and they were all taken off upon the gun-boats, and carried down to Beaufort.

"I nebber see such a sight," said Harriet; we laughed, an' laughed, an' laughed. Here you'd see a woman wid a pail on her head, rice a smokin' in it jus as she'd taken it from de fire, young one hangin' on behind, one han' roun' her forehead to hold on, 'tother han' diggin' into de rice-pot, eatin' wid all its might; hold of her dress two or three more; down her back a bag wid a pig in it. One woman brought two pigs, a white one, an' a black one; we took 'em all on board; named de white pig Beauregard, an' de black pig Jeff Davis. Sometimes de women would come wid twins hangin' roun' der necks; 'pears like I nebber see so many twins in my life; bags on der shoulders, baskets on der heads, and young ones taggin' behin', all loaded; pigs squealin', chickens screamin', young ones squallin'." And so they came pouring down to the gun-boats. When they stood on the shore, and the small boats put out to take them off, they all wanted to get in at once. After the boats were crowded, they would hold on to them so that they could not leave the shore. The oarsmen would beat them on their hands, but they would not let go; they were afraid the gun-boats would go off and leave them, and all wanted to make sure of one of these arks of refuge. At length Col. Montgomery shouted from the upper deck, above the clamor of appealing tones, "Moses, you'll have to give 'em a song." Then Harriet lifted up her voice and sang:

> "Of all the whole creation in the east or in the west,
> The glorious Yankee nation is the greatest and the best.
> Come along! Come along! don't be alarmed,
> Uncle Sam is rich enough to give you all a farm."

At the end of every verse, the negroes in their enthusiasm would throw up their hands and shout

"Glory," and the row-boats would take that opportunity to push off; and so at last they were all brought on board. The masters fled; houses and barns and railroad bridges were burned, tracks torn up, torpedoes destroyed, and the expedition was in all respects successful.

This fearless woman was often sent into the rebel lines as a spy, and brought back valuable information as to the position of armies and batteries; she has been in battle when the shot was falling like hail, and the bodies of dead and wounded men were dropping around her like leaves in autumn; but the thought of fear never seems to have had place for a moment in her mind. She had her duty to perform, and she expected to be taken care of till it was done.

Would that instead of taking them in this poor way at second-hand, my readers could hear this woman's graphic accounts of scenes she herself witnessed, could listen to her imitations of negro preachers in their own very peculiar dialect, her singing of camp-meeting hymns, her account of "experience meetings," her imitations of the dances, and the funeral ceremonies of these simple people. "Why, der language down dar in de far South is jus' as different from ours in Maryland, as you can think," said she. "Dey laughed when dey heard me talk, an' I could not understand dem, no how." She described a midnight funeral which she attended; for the slaves, never having been allowed to bury their dead in the day time, continued the custom of night funerals from habit.

The corpse was laid upon the ground, and the people all sat round, the group being lighted up by pine torches.

The old negro preacher began by giving out a hymn, which was sung by all. "An' oh! I wish you could hear 'em sing, Missus," said Harriet. "Der voices is so sweet, and dey can sing eberyting we sing, an' den dey can sing a great many hymns dat we can't nebber catch at all."

The old preacher began his sermon by pointing to the dead man, who lay in a rude box on the ground before him.

"*Shum?* Ded-a-de-dah! *Shum, David?* Ded-a-de-dah! Now I want you all to *flec'* for moment. Who ob all dis congregation is gwine next to lie ded-a-de-dah? You can't go nowheres, my frien's and bredren, but Deff 'll fin' you. You can't dig no hole so deep an' bury yourself dar, but God A'mighty's far-seein' eye 'll fine you, an' Deff 'll come arter you. You can't go into that big fort (pointing to Hilton Head), an' shut yourself up dar; dat fort dat Sesh Buckner said de debil couldn't take, but Deff 'll fin' you dar. All your frien's may forget you, but Deff 'll nebber forget you. Now, my bredren, prepare to lie ded-a-de-dah!"

This was the burden of a very long sermon, after which the whole congregation went round in a sort of solemn dance, called the "spiritual shuffle," shaking hands with each other, and calling each other by name as they sang:

My sis'r Mary 's boun' to go;
My sis'r Nanny 's boun' to go;
My brudder Tony 's boun' to go;
My brudder July 's boun' to go.

This to the same tune, till every hand had been shaken by every one of the company. When they came to Harriet, who was a stranger, they sang:

Eberybody 's boun' to go!

The body was then placed in a Government wagon, and by the light of the pine torches, the strange, dark procession moved along, singing a rude funeral hymn, till they reached the place of burial.

Harriet's account of her interview with an old negro she met at Hilton Head, is amusing and interesting. He said, "I'd been yere seventy-three years, workin' for my master widout even a dime wages. I'd worked rain-wet sun dry. I'd worked wid my mouf full of dust, but would not stop to get a drink of water. I'd been whipped, an' starved, an' I was always prayin', 'Oh! Lord, come an' delibber us!' All dat time de birds had been flyin', an' de rabens had been cryin', and de fish had been sunnin' in de waters. One day I look up, an' I see a big cloud; it didn't come up like as de clouds come out far yonder, but it 'peared to be right ober head. Der was tunders out of dat, an' der was lightnin's. Den I looked down on de water, an' I see, 'peared to me a big house in de water, an' out of de big house came great big eggs, and de good eggs went on trou' de air, an' fell into de fort; an' de bad eggs burst before dey got dar. Den de Sesh Buckra begin to run, an de neber stop running till de git to de swamp, an' de stick dar an' de die dar. Den I heard 'twas the Yankee ship* firin' out de big eggs, an dey had come to set us free. Den I praise de Lord. He come an' put he little finger in de work, an' dey Sesh Buckra all go; and de birds stop flyin', and de rabens stop cryin', an' when I go to catch a fish to eat wid my rice, de 's no fish dar. De Lord A'mighty 'd come and frightened 'em all

* The Wabash.

out of de waters. Oh! Praise de Lord! I 'd prayed seventy-three years, an' now he 's come an' we's all free."

The last time Harriet was returning from the war, with her pass as hospital nurse, she bought a half-fare ticket, as she was told she must do; and missing the other train, she got into an emigrant train on the Amboy Railroad. When the conductor looked at her ticket, he said, "Come, hustle out of here! We don't carry niggers for half-fare." Harriet explained to him that she was in the employ of Government, and was entitled to transportation as the soldiers were. But the conductor took her forcibly by the arm, and said, "I'll make you tired of trying to stay here." She resisted, and being very strong, she could probably have got the better of the conductor, had he not called three men to his assistance. The car was filled with emigrants, and no one seemed to take her part. The only words she heard, accompanied with fearful oaths, were, "Pitch the nagur out!" They nearly wrenched her arm off, and at length threw her, with all their strength, into a baggage-car. She supposed her arm was broken, and in intense suffering she came on to New York. As she left the car, a delicate-looking young man came up to her, and, handing her a card, said, "You ought to sue that conductor, and if you want a witness, call on me." Harriet remained all winter under the care of a physician in New York; he advised her to sue the Railroad company, and said that he would willingly testify as to her injuries. But the card the young man had given her was only a visiting card, and she did not know where to find him, and so she let the matter go.

The writer here finds it necessary to apologize for the very desultory and hasty manner in which this little book is written. Being herself pressed for time, in the expectation of soon leaving the country, she is obliged to pen down the material to be used in the short and interrupted interviews she can obtain with Harriet, and also to use such letters and accounts as may be sent her, as they come, without being able to work them in, in the order of time. A very material assistance is to be rendered her by the kind offer of an account of Harriet's services during the war, written by Mr. Charles P. Wood, of Auburn, and kindly copied by one of Harriet's most faithful and most efficient friends, Mrs. S. M. Hopkins, of that place.

It was a wise plan of our sagacious heroine to leave her old parents till the last to be brought away. They were pensioned off as too old to work, had a cabin, and a horse and cow, and were quite comfortable. If Harriet had taken them away before the young people, these last would have been sold into Southern slavery, to keep them out of her way. But at length Harriet heard that the old man had been betrayed by a slave whom he had assisted, but who had turned back, and when questioned by his wife, told her the story of his intended escape, and of the aid he had received from "Old Ben." This woman, hoping to curry favor with her master, revealed the whole to him, and "Old Ben" was arrested. He was to be tried the next week, when Harriet appeared upon the scene, and, as she says, "saved dem de expense ob de trial, and removed her father to a higher court, by taking him off to Canada. The manner of their escape is detailed in the following letter from Thomas Garrett, the Wilmington Quaker:

WILMINGTON, 6th Mo., 1868.

MY FRIEND: Thy favor of the 12th reached me yesterday, requesting such reminiscences as I could give respecting the remarkable labors of Harriet Tubman, in aiding her colored friends from bondage. I may begin by saying, living as I have in a slave State, and the laws being very severe where any proof could be made of any one aiding slaves on their way to freedom, I have not felt at liberty to keep any written word of Harriet's or my own labors, except in numbering those whom I have aided. For that reason I cannot furnish so interesting an account of Harriet's labors as I otherwise could, and now would be glad to do; for in truth I never met with any person, of any color, who had more confidence in the voice of God, as spoken direct to her soul. She has frequently told me that she talked with God, and he talked with her every day of her life, and she has declared to me that she felt no more fear of being arrested by her former master, or any other person, when in his immediate neighborhood, than she did in the State of New York, or Canada, for she said she never ventured only where God sent her, and her faith in a Supreme Power truly was great.

I have now been confined to my room with indisposition more than four weeks, and cannot sit to write much; but I feel so much interested in Harriet that I will try to give some of the most remarkable incidents that now present themselves to my mind. The date of the commencement of her labors, I cannot certainly give; but I think it must have been about 1845; from that time till 1860, I think she must have brought from the neighborhood where she had been held as a slave, from 60 to 80 persons, from Maryland, some 80 miles from here. No slave who placed himself under her care, was ever arrested that I have heard of; she mostly had her regular stopping places on her route; but in one instance, when she had two stout men with her, some 30 miles below here, she said that God told her to stop, which she did; and then asked him what she must do. He told her to leave the road, and turn to the left; she obeyed, and soon came to a small stream of tide water; there was no boat, no bridge; she again inquired of her Guide what she was to do. She was told to go through. It was cold, in the month of March; but having confidence in her Guide, she went in; the water came up to her arm-pits; the men refused to follow till they saw her safe on the opposite shore. They then followed, and if I mistake not, she had soon to wade a second stream; soon after which she came to a cabin of colored people, who took them all in, put them to bed, and dried their clothes, ready to proceed next night on their journey. Harriet had run out of money, and gave them some of her underclothing to pay for their kindness. When she called on me two days after, she was so hoarse she could hardly speak, and was also suffering with violent toothache. The strange part of the story we found to be, that the master of these two men had put up the previous day, at the railroad station near where she left, an advertisement for them, offering a large reward for their apprehension; but they made a safe exit. She at one time brought as many as seven or eight, several of whom were women and children. She was well known here in Chester County and Philadelphia, and respected by all true abolitionists. I had been in the habit of furnishing her and those that accompanied her, as she returned from her acts of mercy, with new shoes; and on one occasion when I had not seen her for three months, she came into my store. I said, "Harriet, I am glad to see thee! I suppose thee wants a pair of new shoes." Her reply was "I want more than that." I, in jest, said, "I have always been liberal with thee, and wish to be; but I am not rich, and cannot afford to give much." Her reply was: "God tells me you have money for me." I asked her "if God never deceived her?" She said, "No!" "Well! how much does thee want?" After studying a moment, she said: "About twenty-three dollars." I then gave her twenty-four dollars and some odd cents, the net proceeds of five pounds sterling, received through Eliza Wigham, of Scotland, for her. I had given some accounts of Harriet's labor to the Anti-Slavery Society of Edinburgh, of which Eliza Wigham was Secretary. On the reading of my letter, a gentleman present said he would send Harriet four pounds if he knew of any way to get it to her. Eliza Wigham offered to forward it to me for her, and that was the first money ever received by me for her. Some twelve months after, she called on me again, and said that God told her I had some money for her, but not so much as before. I had, a few days previous, received the net proceeds of one pound ten shillings from Europe for her. To say the least, there was something remarkable in these facts, whether clairvoyance, or the divine impression on her mind from the source of all power, I cannot tell; but certain it was she had a guide within herself other than the written word, for she never had any education. She brought away her aged parents in a singular manner. They started with an old horse, fitted out in primitive style with a *straw collar*, a pair of old chaise wheels, with a board on the axle to sit on, another board swung with ropes, fastened to the axle, to rest their feet on. She got her parents, who were both slaves belonging to different masters, on this rude vehicle to the railroad, put them in the cars, turned Jehu herself, and drove to town in a style that no human being ever did before or since; but she was happy at having arrived safe. Next day, I furnished her with money to take them all to Canada. I afterwards sold their horse, and sent them the balance of the proceeds. I believe that Harriet succeeded in freeing all her relatives but one sister and her three children. Etc., etc. Thy friend,

THOS. GARRETT.

Friend Garrett probably refers here to those who passed through his hands. Harriet was obliged to come by many different routes on her different journeys, and though she never counted those whom she brought away with her, it would seem, by the computation of others, that there must have been somewhere near three hundred brought by her to the Northern States and Canada.

Extracts from a letter written by Mr. Sanborn, Secretary of the Massachusetts Board of State Charities.

MY DEAR MADAME: Mr. Phillips has sent me your note, asking for reminiscences of Harriet Tubman, and testimonials to her extraordinary story, which all her New England friends will, I am sure, be glad to furnish.

I never had reason to doubt the truth of what Harriet said in regard to her own career, for I found her singularly truthful. Her imagination is warm and rich, and there is a whole region of the marvelous in her nature, which has manifested itself at times remarkably. Her dreams and visions, misgivings and forewarnings, ought not to be omitted in any life of her, particularly those relating to John Brown.

She was in his confidence in 1858–9, and he had a great regard for her, which he often expressed to me. She aided him in his plans, and expected to do so still further, when his career was closed by that wonderful campaign in Virginia. The first time she came to my house, in Concord, after that tragedy, she was shown into a room in the evening, where Brackett's bust of John Brown was standing. The sight of it, which was new to her, threw her into a sort of ecstacy of sorrow and admiration, and she went on in her rhapsodical way to pronounce his apotheosis.

She has often been in Concord, where she resided at the houses of Emerson, Alcott, the Whitneys, the Brooks family, Mrs. Horace Mann, and other well known persons. They all admired and respected her, and nobody doubted the reality of her adventures. She was too *real* a person to be suspected. In 1862, I think it was, she went from Boston to Port Royal, under the advice and encouragement of Mr. Garrison, Governor Andrew, Dr. Howe, and other leading people. Her career in South Carolina is well known to some of our officers, and I think to Colonel Higginson, now of Newport, R. I., and Colonel James Montgomery, of Kansas, to both of whom she was useful as a spy and guide, if I mistake not. I regard her as, on the whole, the most extraordinary person of her race I have ever met. She is a negro of pure or almost pure blood, can neither read nor write, and has the characteristics of her race and condition. But she has done what can scarcely be credited on the best authority, and she has accomplished her purposes with a coolness, foresight, patience, and wisdom, which in a *white man* would have raised him to the highest pitch of reputation.

I am, dear Madame, very truly your servant,

F. B. Sanborn.

Of the "dreams and visions" mentioned in this

letter, the writer might have given many wonderful instances; but it was thought best not to insert anything which, with any, might bring discredit upon the story. When these turns of somnolency come upon Harriet, she imagines that her "spirit" leaves her body, and visits other scenes and places, not only in this world, but in the world of spirits. And her ideas of these scenes show, to say the least of it, a vividness of imagination seldom equaled in the soarings of the most cultivated minds.

Not long since, the writer, on going into Harriet's room in the morning, sat down by her and began to read that wonderful and glorious description of the heavenly Jerusalem in the two last chapters of Revelations. When the reading was finished, Harriet burst into a rhapsody which perfectly amazed her hearer—telling of what she had seen in one of these visions, sights which no one could doubt had been real to her, and which no human imagination could have conceived, it would seem, unless in dream or vision. There was a wild poetry in these descriptions which seemed to border almost on inspiration, but by many they might be characterized as the ravings of insanity. All that can be said is, however, if this woman is insane, there has been a wonderful "method in her madness."

At one time, Harriet was much troubled in spirit about her three brothers, feeling sure that some great evil was impending over their heads. She wrote a letter, by the hand of a friend, to a man named Jacob Jackson, who lived near there. Jacob was a free negro, who could both read and write, and who was under suspicion at that time, as it was thought he had something to do with the disappearance of so many slaves. It was necessary, therefore, to be very cautious in writing to him. Jacob had an adopted son, William Henry Jackson, also free, who had come South; and so Harriet determined to sign her letter with his name, knowing that Jacob would be clever enough to understand, by her peculiar phraseology, what meaning she intended to convey to him. She, therefore, after speaking of indifferent matters, said, "Read my letter to the old folks, and give my love to them, and tell my brothers to be always *watching unto prayer*, and when the *good old ship of Zion comes along, to be ready to step aboard.*"

The letter was signed "William Henry Jackson." Jacob was not allowed to have his letters till the self-elected inspectors had had the reading of them, and studied into their secret meaning.

They, therefore, got together, wiped their glasses, and got them on, and proceeded to a careful perusal of this mysterious document. What it meant, they could not imagine; William Henry Jackson had no parents or brothers, and the letter was incomprehensible. White genius having exhausted itself, black genius was called in, and Jacob's letter was at last handed to him. Jacob saw at once what it meant, but tossed it down, saying, "Dat letter can't be meant for me, no how. I can't make head nor tail of it," and walked off and took immediate measures to let Harriet's brothers know secretly that she was coming, and they must be ready to start at a moment's notice for the North. When Harriet arrived there, it was the day before Christmas, and she found her three brothers, who had attempted to escape, were advertised to be sold on Christmas day to the highest bidder, to go down to the cotton and rice fields with the chain-gang. Christmas came on Sunday, and therefore they were not to be sold till Monday. Harriet arrived on Saturday, and gave them secret notice to be ready to start Saturday night, immediately after dark, the first stopping-place to be their father's cabin, forty miles away. When they assembled, their brother John was missing; but when Harriet was ready, the word was "Forward!" and she "nebber waited for no one." Poor John was almost ready to start, when his wife was taken ill, and in an hour or two, another little inheritor of the blessings of slavery had come into the world. John must go off for a "Granny," and then he would not leave his wife in her present circumstances. But after the birth of the child, he began to think he must start; the North and Liberty, or the South and life-long Slavery— these were the alternatives, and this was his last chance. He tried again and again to steal out of the door, but a watchful eye was on him, and he was always arrested by the question, "Where you gwine, John?" At length he told her he was going to try to see if he couldn't get hired out on Christmas to another man. His wife did not think that he was to be sold. He went out of the door, and stood by the corner of the house, near her bed, listening. At length, he heard her sobbing and crying, and not being able to endure it, he went back. "Oh! John," said his wife, "you's gwine to lebe me; but, wherebber you go, remember me an' de chillen." John went out and started at full speed for his father's cabin, forty miles away. At daybreak, he overtook the others in the "fodder house," near the cabin of their parents. Harriet had not seen her mother there for six years, but they did not dare to let the old woman know of their being in her neighborhood, or of their intentions, for she would have raised such an uproar in her efforts to detain them with her, that the whole plantation would have been alarmed. The poor old woman had been expecting the boys all day, to spend Christmas with her as usual. She had been hard at work, had killed a pig, and put it to all the various uses to which sinner's flesh is doomed, and had made all the preparations her circumstances admitted of, to give them a sumptuous entertainment, and there she sat watching. In the night, when Harriet and two of her brothers and two other men, who had escaped with them, arrived at the "fodder house," they were exhausted and famished. They sent the two strange men up to the house to try and speak to "Old Ben," their father, but not to let their mother know of their being in the neighborhood. The men succeeded in rousing old Ben, who came out, and as soon as he heard their story, he gathered together a quantity of provisions, and came down to the fodder house, and slipped them inside the door, taking care not to *see* his children.

Up among the ears of corn they lay, and one of them he had not seen for six years. It rained very hard all that Sunday, and there they lay all day, for they could not start till night. At about daybreak, John joined them. There were wide chinks in the boards of the fodder house, and through them they could see their father's cabin; and all day long, every few minutes, they would see the old woman come out, and, shading her eyes with her hand, take a long look down the road to see if her children were coming, and then they could almost hear her sigh as she turned into the house, disappointed.

Two or three times the old man came down, and pushed food inside the door, and after nightfall he came to accompany them part of the way upon their journey. When he reached the fodder house, he tied his handkerchief tight over his eyes, and two of his sons taking him by each arm, he accompanied them some miles upon their' journey. They then bade him farewell, and left him standing blind-fold in the middle of the road. When he could no longer hear their footsteps, he took off the handkerchief, and turned back.

But before leaving, they had gone up to the cabin

to take a silent farewell of the poor old mother. Through the little window of the cabin, they saw the old woman sitting by her fire with a pipe in her mouth, her head on her hand, rocking back and forth as she did when she was in tιouble, and wondering what new evil had come to her children. With streaming eyes, they watched her for ten or fifteen minutes; but time was precious, and they must reach their next station before daybreak, and so they turned sadly away.

When the holidays were over, and the men came for the three brothers to sell them, they could not be found. The first place to search was of course the plantation where all their relatives and friends lived. They went to the "big house," and asked the "Doctor" if he had seen anything of them. The Doctor said, "No, they mostly came up there to see the other niggers when they came for Christmas, but they hadn't been round at all. "Have you been down to Old Ben's?" the Doctor asked. "Yes." "What does Old Rit say?" "Old Rit says not one of 'em came this Christmas. She was looking for 'em most all day, and most broke her heart about it." "What does Old Ben say?" "Old Ben says that he hasn't seen one of his children this Christmas." "Well, if Old Ben says that, they haven't been round." And so the man-hunters went off disappointed.

One of the other brothers, William Henry, had long been attached to a girl named Catherine, who lived with another master; but her master would not let her marry him. When William Henry made up his mind to start with Harriet, he determined to bring Catherine with him. And so he went to a tailor's, and bought a new suit of men's clothes, and threw them over the garden fence of Catherine's master. The garden ran down to a run, and Catherine had been notified where to find the clothes. When the time had come to get ready, Catherine went to the foot of the garden and dressed herself in the suit of men's clothes. She was soon missed, and all the girls in the house were set to looking for Catherine. Presently they saw coming up through the garden, as if from the river, a well-dressed little darkey, and they all stopped looking for Catherine to stare at him. He walked directly by them round the house, and went out of the gate, without the slightest suspicion being excited as to who he was. In a fortnight from that time, the whole party were safe in Canada.

William Henry died in Canada, but Catherine

has been seen and talked with by the writer, at the house of the old people.

Of the many letters, testimonials, and passes, placed in the hands of the writer by Harriet, the following are selected for insertion in this book, and are quite sufficient to verify her statements.

A Letter from Gen. Saxton to a Lady of Auburn.

ATLANTA, GA., March 21, 1868.

MY DEAR MADAME: I have just received your letter informing me that Hon. Wm. H. Seward, Secretary of State, would present a petition to Congress for a pension to Harriet Tubman, for services rendered in the Union Army during the late war. I can bear witness to the value of her services in South Carolina and Florida. She was employed in the hospitals and as a spy. She made many a raid inside the enemy's lines, displaying remarkable courage, zeal, and fidelity. She was employed by General Hunter, and I think by Generals Stevens and Sherman, and is as deserving of a pension from the Government for her services as any other of its faithful servants.

I am very truly yours,

RUFUS SAXTON, Bvt. Brig.-Gen. U. S. A.

Letter from Hon. Wm. H. Seward.

WASHINGTON, July 25, 1868.

MAJ.-GEN. HUNTER—

MY DEAR SIR: Harriet Tubman, a colored woman, has been nursing our soldiers during nearly all the war. She believes she has a claim for faithful services to the command in South Carolina with which you are connected, and she thinks that you would be disposed to see her claim justly settled.

I have known her long, and a nobler, higher spirit, or a truer, seldom dwells in the human form. I commend her, therefore, to your kind and best attentions. Faithfully your friend,

WILLIAM H. SEWARD.

Letter from Col. James Montgomery.

ST. HELENA ISLAND, S. C., July 6, 1863.
HEADQUARTERS COLORED BRIGADE.

BRIG.-GEN. GILMAN, Commanding Department of the South—

GENERAL: I wish to commend to your attention, Mrs. Harriet Tubman, a most remarkable woman, and invaluable as a scout. I have been acquainted with her character and actions for several years.

Walter D. Plowden is a man of tried courage, and can be made highly useful.

I am, General, your most ob't servant,

JAMES MONTGOMERY, Col. Com. Brigade.

Letter from Mrs. Gen. A. Baird.

PETERBORO, Nov. 24, 1864.

The bearer of this, Harriet Tubman, a most excellent woman, who has rendered faithful and good services to our Union army, not only in the hospital, but in various capacities, having been employed under Government at Hilton Head, and in Florida; and I commend her to the protection of all officers in whose department she may happen to be.

She has been known and esteemed for years by the family of my uncle, Hon. Gerrit Smith, as a person of great rectitude and capabilities.

MRS. GEN. A. BAIRD.

Letter from Hon. Gerrit Smith.

PETERBORO, N. Y., Nov. 4, 1867.

I have known Mrs. Harriet Tubman for many years. Seldom, if ever, have I met with a person more philanthropic, more self-denying, and of more bravery. Nor must I omit to say that she combines with her sublime spirit, remarkable discernment and judgment.

During the late war, Mrs. Tubman was eminently faithful and useful to the cause of our country. She is poor and has poor parents. Such a servant of the country should be well paid by the country. I hope that the Government will look into her case. GERRIT SMITH.

Testimonial from Gerrit Smith.

PETERBORO, Nov. 22, 1864.

The bearer, Harriet Tubman, needs not any recommendation. Nearly all the nation over, she has been heard of for her wisdom, integrity, patriotism, and bravery. The cause of freedom owes her much. The country owes her much.

I have known Harriet for many years, and I hold her in my high esteem. GERRIT SMITH.

Certificate from Henry K. Durrant, Acting Asst. Surgeon, U. S. A.

I certify that I have been acquainted with Harriet Tubman for nearly two years; and my position as Medical Officer in charge of "contrabands" in this town and in hospital, has given me frequent and ample opportunities to observe her general deportment; particularly her kindness and attention to the sick and suffering of her own race. I take much pleasure in testifying to the esteem in which she is generally held.

HENRY K. DURRANT,
Acting Assistant Surgeon, U. S. A.
In charge "Contraband" Hospital.

Dated at Beaufort, S. C., the 3d day of May, 1864.

I concur fully in the above.

R. SAXTON, Brig.-Gen. Vol.

The following are a few of the passes used by Harriet throughout the war. Many others are so defaced that it is impossible to decipher them.

HEADQUARTERS DEPARTMENT OF THE SOUTH,
HILTON HEAD, PORT ROYAL, S. C., Feb. 19, 1863.

Pass the bearer, Harriet Tubman, to Beaufort and back to this place, and wherever she wishes to go; and give her free passage at all times, on all Government transports. Harriet was sent to me from

Boston by Gov. Andrew of Mass., and is a valuable woman. She has permission, as a servant of the Government, to purchase such provisions from the Commissary as she may need.

D. HUNTER, Maj.-Gen. Com.

General Gillman, who succeeded General Hunter in command of the Department of the South, appends his signature to the same pass.

HEADQUARTERS OF THE DEPARTMENT OF THE SOUTH,
July 1, 1863.

Continued in force.

I. A. GILLMAN, Brig.-Gen. Com.

BEAUFORT, Aug. 28, 1862.

Will Capt. Warfield please let "Moses" have a little Bourbon whiskey for medicinal purposes.

HENRY K. DURRANT, Act. Ass. Surgeon.

WAR DEPARTMENT, WASHINGTON, D. C.,
March 20, 1865.

Pass Mrs. Harriet Tubman (colored) to Hilton Head and Charleston, S. C., with free transportation on a Government transport.

By order of the Sec. of War.

LOUIS H., Asst. Adj.-Gen., U. S. A.

To Bvt. Brig.-Gen. Van Vliet, U. S. Q. M., N. Y.

Not transferable.

WAR DEPARTMENT, WASHINGTON, D. C.,
July 22, 1865.

Permit Harriet Tubman to proceed to Fortress Monroe, Va., on a Government transport. Transportation will be furnished free of cost.

By order of the Secretary of War.

L. H., Asst. Adj.-Gen.

Not transferable.

Appointment as Nurse.

SIR:—I have the honor to inform you that the Medical Director Department of Virginia has been instructed to appoint Harriet Tubman nurse or matron at the Colored Hospital, Fort Monroe, Va.

Very respectfully, your obdt. servant,

V. K. BARNES, Surgeon-General.

Hon. WM. H. SEWARD,
Secretary of State, Washington, D. C.

Names of Harriet's Assistants, Scouts, or Pilots.

Scouts who are residents of Beaufort, and well acquainted with the main land: Peter Barns, Mott Blake, Sandy Selters, Solomon Gregory, Isaac Hayward, Gabriel Cohen, George Chrisholm.

Pilots who know the channels of the rivers in this vicinity, and who acted as such for Col. Montgomery up the Combahee River: Charles Simmons, Samuel Hayward.

App'd, R. SAXTON, Brig.-Gen.

At this point the following good and kind letter from Rev. Henry Fowler is received:

AUBURN, June 23, 1868.

MY DEAR FRIEND:—I wish to say to you how gratified I am that you are writing the biography of Harriet Tubman. I feel that her life forms part of the history of the country, and that it ought not to depend upon tradition to keep it in remembrance. Had not the pressure of professional claims prevented, I should have aspired to be her historian myself; but my disappointment in this regard is more than met by the satisfaction experienced in hearing that you are the chosen Miriam of this African "Moses;" the name by which she was known among her emancipated followers from the land of bondage. Blessed be God! a "Greater than Moses" has at last broken every bond.

As ever, with warm regard, your friend,

HENRY FOWLER.

The following account of the subject of this memoir is cut from the *Boston Commonwealth* of 1863, kindly sent the writer by Mr. Sanborn:

"It was said long ago that the true romance of America was not in the fortunes of the Indian, where Cooper sought it, nor in the New England character, where Judd found it, nor in the social contrasts of Virginia planters, as Thackeray imagined, but in the story of the fugitive slaves. The observation is as true now as it was before war, with swift, gigantic hand, sketched the vast shadows, and dashed in the high lights in which romance loves to lurk and flash forth. But the stage is enlarged on which these dramas are played, the whole world now sit as spectators, and the desperation or the magnanimity of a poor black woman has power to shake the nation that so long was deaf to her cries. We write of one of these heroines, of whom our slave annals are full,—a woman whose career is as extraordinary as the most famous of her sex can show.

"Araminta Ross, now known by her married name of Tubman, with her sounding Christian name changed to Harriet, is the grand-daughter of a slave imported from Africa, and has not a drop of white blood in her veins. Her parents were Benjamin Ross and Harriet Greene, both slaves, but married and faithful to each other. They still live in old age and poverty, but free, on a little property at Auburn, N. Y., which their daughter purchased for them from Mr. Seward, the Secretary of State. She was born, as near as she can remember, in 1820 or in 1821, in Dorchester County, on the Eastern shore of Maryland, and not far from the town of Cambridge. She had ten brothers and sisters, of whom three are now living, all at the North, and all rescued from slavery by Harriet, before the War. She went back just as the South was preparing to secede, to bring away a fourth, but before she could reach her, she was dead. Three years before, she had brought away her old father and mother, at great risk to herself.

"When Harriet was six years old, she was taken from her mother and carried ten miles to live with James Cook, whose wife was a weaver, to learn the trade of weaving. While still a mere child, Cook set her to watching his musk-rat traps, which compelled her to wade through the water. It happened that she was once sent when she was ill with the measles, and, taking cold from wading in the water in this condition, she grew very sick, and her mother persuaded her master to take her away from Cook's until she could get well.

"Another attempt was made to teach her weaving, but she would not learn, for she hated her mistress, and did not want to live at home, as she would have done as a weaver, for it was the custom then to weave the cloth for the family, or a part of it, in the house.

"Soon after she entered her teens she was hired out as a field hand, and it was while thus employed that she received a wound which nearly proved fatal, from the effects of which she still suffers. In the fall of the year, the slaves there work in the evening, cleaning up wheat, husking corn, etc. On this occasion, one of the slaves of a farmer named Barrett, left his work, and went to the village store in the evening. The overseer followed him, and so did Harriet. When the slave was found, the overseer swore he should be whipped, and called on Harriet, among others, to help tie him. She refused, and as the man ran away, she placed herself in the door to stop pursuit. The overseer caught up a two-pound weight from the counter and threw it at the fugitive, but it fell short and struck Harriet a stunning blow on the head. It was long before she recovered from this, and it has left her subject to a sort of stupor or lethargy at times; coming upon her in the midst of conversation, or whatever she may be doing, and throwing her into a deep slumber, from which she will presently rouse herself, and go on with her conversation or work.

"After this she lived for five or six years with John Stewart, where at first she worked in the house, but afterwards 'hired her time,' and Dr. Thompson, son of her master's guardian, 'stood for her,' that is, was her surety for the payment of what she owed. She employed the time thus hired in the rudest labors,—drove oxen, carted, plowed, and did all the work of a man,—sometimes earning money enough in a year, beyond what she paid her master, 'to buy a pair of steers,' worth forty dollars. The amount exacted of a woman for her time was fifty or sixty dollars,—of a man, one hundred to one hundred and fifty dollars. Frequently Harriet worked for her father, who was a timber inspector, and superintended the cutting and hauling of great quantities of timber for the Baltimore ship-yards. Stewart, his temporary master, was a builder, and for the work of Ross used to receive as much as five dollars a day sometimes, he being a superior workman. While engaged with her father, she would cut wood, haul logs, etc. Her usual 'stint' was half a cord of wood in a day.

"Harriet was married somewhere about 1844, to a free colored man named John Tubman, but she had no children. For the last two years of slavery she lived with Dr. Thompson, before mentioned, her own master not being yet of age, and Dr. T.'s father being his guardian, as well as the owner of her own father. In 1849 the young man died, and the slaves were to be sold, though previously set free by an old will. Harriet resolved not to be sold, and so, with no knowledge of the North—having only heard of Pennsylvania and New Jersey—she walked away one night alone. She found a friend in a white lady, who knew her story and helped her on her way. After many adventures, she reached Philadelphia, where she found work and earned a small stock of money. With this money in her purse, she traveled back to Maryland for her husband, but she found him married to another woman, and no longer caring to live with her. This, however, was not until two years after her escape, for she does not seem to have reached her old home in her first two expeditions. In December, 1850, she had visited Baltimore and brought away her sister and two children, who had come up from Cambridge in a boat, under charge of her sister's husband, a free black. A few months after she had brought away her brother and two other men, but it was not till the fall of 1851 that she found her husband and learned of his infidelity. She did not give way to rage or grief, but collected a party of fugitives and brought them safely to Philadelphia. In December of the same year, she returned, and led out a party of eleven, among them her brother and his wife. With these she journeyed to Canada, and there spent the winter, for this was after the enforcement of Mason's Fugitive Slave Bill in Philadelphia and Boston, and there was no safety except 'under the paw of the British Lion,' as she quaintly said. But the first winter was terribly severe for these poor runaways. They earned their bread by chopping wood in the snows of a Canadian forest; they were frost-bitten, hungry, and naked. Harriet was their good angel. She kept house for her brother, and the poor creatures boarded with her. She worked for them, begged for them, prayed for them, with the strange familiarity of communion with God which seems natural to these people, and carried them by the help of God through the hard winter.

"In the spring she returned to the States, and as usual earned money by working in hotels and families as a cook. From Cape May, in the fall of 1852, she went back once more to Maryland, and brought away nine more fugitives.

"Up to this time she had expended chiefly her own money in these expeditions—money which she had earned by hard work in the drudgery of the kitchen. Never did any one more exactly fulfill the sense of George Herbert—

"A servant with this clause
Makes drudgery divine."

"But it was not possible for such virtues long to remain hidden from the keen eyes of the Abolitionists. She became known to Thomas Garrett, the large-hearted Quaker of Wilmington, who has aided the escape of three thousand fugitives; she found warm friends in Philadelphia and New York, and wherever she went. These gave her money, which she never spent for her own use, but laid up for the help of her people, and especially for her journeys back to the 'land of Egypt,' as she called her old home. By reason of her frequent visits there, always carrying away some of the oppressed, she got among her people the name of 'Moses,' which it seems she still retains.

"Between 1852 and 1857, she made but two of these journeys, in consequence partly of the increased vigilance of the slaveholders, who had suffered so much by the loss of their property. A great reward was offered for her capture, and she several times was on the point of being taken, but always escaped by her quick wit, or by 'warnings' from Heaven—for it is time to notice one singular trait in her character. She is the most shrewd and practical person in the world, yet she is a firm believer in omens, dreams, and warnings. She declares that before her escape from slavery, she used to dream of flying over fields and towns, and rivers and mountains, looking down upon them 'like a bird,' and reaching at last a great fence, or sometimes a river, over which she would try to fly, 'but it 'peared like I wouldn't hab de strength, and jes as I was sinkin' down, dare would be ladies all drest in white ober dere, and dey would put out dere arms and pull me 'cross.' There is nothing strange in this, perhaps, but she declares that when she came North she remembered these very places as those she had seen in her dreams, and many of the ladies who befriended her were those she had been helped by in her visions.

"Then she says she always knows when there is

danger near her,—she does not know how, exactly, but "'pears like my heart go flutter, flutter, and den dey may say "Peace, Peace," as much as dey likes, *I know its gwine to be war!*" She is very firm on this point, and ascribes to this her great impunity, in spite of the lethargy before mentioned, which would seem likely to throw her into the hands of her enemies. She says she inherited this power, that her father could always predict the weather, and that he foretold the Mexican war.

"In 1867 she made her most venturesome journey, for she brought with her to the North her old parents, who were no longer able to walk such distances as she must go by night. Consequently she must hire a wagon for them, and it required all her ingenuity to get them through Maryland and Delaware safe. She accomplished it, however, and by the aid of her friends she brought them safe to Canada, where they spent the winter. Her account of their sufferings there—of her mother's complaining and her own philosophy about it—is a lesson of trust in Providence better than many sermons. But she decided to bring them to a more comfortable place, and so she negotiated with Mr. Seward—then in the Senate—for a little patch of ground with a house on it, at Auburn, near his own home.

To the credit of the Secretary of State it should be said, that he sold her the property on very favorable terms, and gave her some time for payment. To this house she removed her parents, and set herself to work to pay for her purchase. It was on this errand that she first visited Boston —we believe in the winter of 1858–9. She brought a few letters from her friends in New York, but she could herself neither read nor write, and she was obliged to trust to her wits that they were delivered to the right persons. One of them, as it happened, was to the present writer, who received it by another hand, and called to see her at her boarding-house. It was curious to see the caution with which she received her visitor until she felt assured that there was no mistake. One of her means of security was to carry with her the daguerreotypes of her friends, and show them to each new person. If they recognized the likeness, then it was all right.

"Pains were taken to secure her the attention to which her great services to humanity entitled her, and she left New England with a handsome sum of money towards the payment of her debt to Mr. Seward. Before she left, however, she had several interviews with Captain Brown, then in Boston.

He is supposed to have communicated his plans to her, and to have been aided by her in obtaining recruits and money among her people. At any rate, he always spoke of her with the greatest respect, and declared that 'General Tubman,' as he styled her, was a better officer than most whom he had seen, and could command an army as successfully as she had led her small parties of fugitives.

"Her own veneration for Captain Brown has always been profound, and since his murder, has taken the form of a religion. She had often risked her own life for her people, and she thought nothing of that; but that a white man, and a man so noble and strong, should so take upon himself the burden of a despised race, she could not understand, and she took refuge from her perplexity in the mysteries of her fervid religion.

"Again, she laid great stress on a dream which she had just before she met Captain Brown in Canada. She thought she was in 'a wilderness sort of place, all full of rocks and bushes,' when she saw a serpent raise its head among the rocks, and as it did so, it became the head of an old man with a long white beard, gazing at her 'wishful like, jes as ef he war gwine to speak to me,' and then two other heads rose up beside him, younger than he,—

and as she stood looking at them, and wondering what they could want with her, a great crowd of men rushed in and struck down the younger heads, and then the head of the old man, still looking at her so 'wishful.' This dream she had again and again, and could not interpret it; but when she met Captain Brown, shortly after, behold, he was the very image of the head she had seen. But still she could not make out what her dream signified, till the news came to her of the tragedy of Harper's Ferry, and then she knew the two other heads were his two sons. She was in New York at that time, and on the day of the affair at Harper's Ferry, she felt her usual warning that something was wrong—she could not tell what. Finally she told her hostess that it must be Captain Brown who was in trouble, and that they should soon hear bad news from him. The next day's newspaper brought tidings of what had happened.

"Her last visit to Maryland was made after this, in December, 1860; and in spite of the agitated condition of the country, and the greater watchfulness of the slaveholders, she brought away seven fugitives, one of them an infant, which must be drugged with opium to keep it from crying on the way, and so revealing the hiding place of the party.

She brought these safely to New York, but there a new difficulty met her. It was the mad winter of compromises, when State after State, and politician after politician, went down on their knees to beg the South not to secede. The hunting of fugitive slaves began again. Mr. Seward went over to the side of compromise. He knew the history of this poor woman; he had given his enemies a hold on him, by dealing with her; it was thought he would not scruple to betray her. The suspicion was an unworthy one, for though the Secretary could betray a cause, he could not surely have put her enemies on the track of a woman who was thus in his power, after such a career as hers had been. But so little confidence was then felt in Mr. Seward, by men who had voted for him and with him, that they hurried Harriet off to Canada, sorely against her will.

"She did not long remain there. The war broke out, for which she had been long looking, and she hastened to her New England friends to prepare for another expedition to Maryland, to bring away the last of her family.

"Before she could start, however, the news came of the capture of Port Royal. Instantly she conceived the idea of going there and working among her people on the islands and the mainland. Money was given her, a pass was secured through the agency of Governor Andrew, and she went to Beaufort. There she has made herself useful in many ways—has been employed as a spy by General Hunter, and finally has piloted Col. Montgomery on his most successful expedition. We gave some notice of this fact last week. Since then we have received the following letter, dictated by her, from which it appears that she needs some contributions for her work. We trust she will receive them, for none has better deserved it. She asks nothing for herself, except that her wardrobe may be replenished, and even this she will probably share with the first needy person she meets.

"'BEAUFORT, S. C., June 30, 1863.

* * * "'Last fall, when the people here became very much alarmed for fear of an invasion from the rebels, all my clothes were packed and sent with others to Hilton Head, and lost; and I have never been able to get any trace of them since. I was sick at the time, and unable to look after them myself. I want, among the rest, a *bloomer* dress, made of some coarse, strong material, to wear on *expeditions*. In our late expedition up the Com-

bahee River, in coming on board the boat, I was carrying *two pigs* for a poor sick woman, who had a child to carry, and the order "double quick" was given, and I started to run, stepped on my dress, it being rather long, and fell and tore it almost off, so that when I got on board the boat, there was hardly anything left of it but shreds. I made up my mind then I would never wear a long dress on another expedition of the kind, but would have a *bloomer* as soon as I could get it. So please make this known to the ladies, if you will, for I expect to have use for it very soon, probably before they can get it to me.

"'You have, without doubt, seen a full account of the expedition I refer to. Don't you think we colored people are entitled to some credit for that exploit, under the lead of the brave Colonel Montgomery? We weakened the rebels somewhat on the Combahee River, by taking and bringing away *seven hundred and fifty-six* head of their most valuable live stock, known up in your region as "contrabands," and this, too, without the loss of a single life on our part, though we had good reason to believe that a number of rebels bit the dust. Of these seven hundred and fifty-six contrabands, nearly or quite all the able-bodied men have joined the colored regiments here.

"'I have now been absent two years almost, and have just got letters from my friends in Auburn, urging me to come home. My father and mother are old and in feeble health, and need my care and attention. I hope the good people there will not allow them to suffer, and I do not believe they will. But I do not see how I am to leave at present the very important work to be done here. Among other duties which I have, is that of looking after the hospital here for contrabands. Most of those coming from the mainland are very destitute, almost naked. I am trying to find places for those able to work, and provide for them as best I can, so as to lighten the burden on the Government as much as possible, while at the same time they learn to respect themselves by earning their own living.

"'Remember me very kindly to Mrs. —— and her daughters; also, if you will, to my Boston friends, Mrs. C., Miss H., and especially to Mr. and Mrs. George L. Stearns, to whom I am under great obligations for their many kindnesses. I shall be sure to come and see you all if I live to go North. If you write, direct your letter to the care of C.'"

In the Spring of 1860, Harriet Tubman was requested by Mr. Gerrit Smith to go to Boston to attend a large Anti-Slavery meeting. On her way, she stopped at Troy to visit a cousin, and while there, the colored people were one day startled with the intelligence that a fugitive slave, by the name of Charles Nalle, had been followed by his master (who was his younger brother, and not one grain whiter than he), and that he was already in the hands of the officers, and was to be taken back to the South. The instant Harriet heard the news, she started for the office of the U. S. Commissioner, scattering the tidings as she went. An excited crowd were gathered about the office, through which Harriet forced her way, and rushed up stairs to the door of the room where the fugitive was detained. A wagon was already waiting before the door to carry off the man, but the crowd was even then so great, and in such a state of excitement, that the officers did not dare to bring the man down. On the opposite side of the street stood the colored people, watching the window where they could see Harriet's sun-bonnet, and feeling assured that so long as she stood there, the fugitive was still in the office. Time passed on, and he did not appear. "They've taken him out another way, depend upon that," said some of the colored people. "No," replied others, "there stands 'Moses' yet, and as long as she is there, he is safe." Harriet, now seeing the necessity for a tremendous effort for his rescue, sent out some little boys to cry *fire*. The bells rang, the crowd increased, till the whole street was a dense mass of people. Again and again the officers came out to try and clear the stairs, and make a way to take their captive down; others were driven down, but Harriet stood her ground, her head bent down, and her arms folded. "Come, old woman, you must get out of this," said one of the officers; "I must have the way cleared; if you can't get down alone, some one will help you." Harriet, still putting on a greater appearance of decrepitude, twitched away from him, and kept her place. Offers were made to buy Charles from his master, who at first agreed to take twelve hundred dollars for him; but when that was subscribed, he immediately raised the price to fifteen hundred. The crowd grew more excited. A gentleman raised a window and called out, "Two hundred dollars for his rescue, but not one cent to his master!" This was responded to by a roar of satisfaction from the crowd below. At length the officers appeared, and announced to the crowd that if they would open a lane to the wagon, they would promise to bring the man down the front way.

The lane was opened, and the man was brought out—a tall, handsome, intelligent *white* man, with his wrists manacled together, walking between the U. S. Marshal and another officer, and behind him his brother and his master, so like him that one could hardly be told from the other. The moment they appeared, Harriet roused from her stooping posture, threw up a window, and cried to her friends: "Here he comes—take him!" and then darted down the stairs like a wild-cat. She seized one officer and pulled him down, then another, and tore him away from the man; and keeping her arms about the slave, she cried to her friends: "Drag us out! Drag him to the river! Drown him! but don't let them have him!" They were knocked down together, and while down she tore off her sun-bonnet and tied it on the head of the fugitive. When he rose, only his head could be seen, and amid the surging mass of people the slave was no longer recognized, while the master appeared like the slave. Again and again they were knocked down, the poor slave utterly helpless, with his manacled wrists streaming with blood.

Harriet's outer clothes were torn from her, and even her stout shoes were all pulled from her feet, yet she never relinquished her hold of the man, till she had dragged him to the river, where he was tumbled into a boat, Harriet fo'lowing in a ferry-boat to the other side. But the telegraph was ahead of them, and as soon as they landed he was seized and hurried from her sight. After a time, some school children came hurrying along, and to her anxious inquiries they answered, "He is up in that house, in the third story." Harriet rushed up to the place. Some men were attempting to make their way up the stairs. The officers were firing down, and two men were lying on the stairs, who had been shot. Over their bodies our heroine rushed, and with the help of others burst open the door of the room, dragged out the fugitive, whom Harriet carried down stairs in her arms. A gentleman who was riding by with a fine horse, stopped to ask what the disturbance meant; and on hearing the story, his sympathies seemed to be thoroughly aroused; he sprang from his wagon, calling out, "That is a blood-horse, drive him till he drops." The poor man was hurried in; some of his friends jumped in after him, and drove at the most rapid rate to Schenectady.

This is the story Harriet told to the writer. By some persons it seemed too wonderful for belief, and an attempt was made to corroborate it. Rev. Henry Fowler, who was at the time at Saratoga, kindly volunteered to go to Troy and ascertain the facts. His report was, that he had had a long interview with Mr. Townsend, who acted during the trial as counsel for the slave, that he had given him a "rich narration," which he would write out the next week for this little book. But before he was to begin his generous labor, and while engaged in some kind efforts for the prisoners at Auburn, he was stricken down by the heat of the sun, and is for a long time debarred from labor.

FUGITIVE SLAVE RESCUE IN TROY.

From the Troy Whig, April 28, 1859.

Yesterday afternoon, the streets of this city and West Troy were made the scenes of unexampled excitement. For the first time since the passage of the Fugitive Slave Law, an attempt was made here to carry its provisions into execution, and the result was a terrific encounter between the officers and the prisoner's friends, the triumph of mob law, and the final rescue of the fugitive. Our city was thrown into a grand state of turmoil, and for a time every other topic was forgotten, to give place to this new excitement. People did not think last evening to ask who was nominated at Charleston, or whether the news of the Heenan and Sayers battle had arrived—everything was merged into the fugitive slave case, of which it seems the end is not yet.

Charles Nalle, the fugitive, who was the cause of all this excitement, was a slave on the plantation of B. W. Hansborough, in Culpepper County, Virginia, till the 19th of October, 1858, when he made his escape, and went to live in Columbia, Pennsylvania. A wife and five children are residing there now. Not long since he came to Sandlake, in this county, and resided in the family of Mr. Crosby until about three weeks ago. Since that time, he has been employed as coachman by Uri Gilbert, Esq., of this city. He is about thirty years of age, tall, quite light-complexioned, and good-looking. He is said to have been an excellent and faithful servant.

At Sandlake, we understand that Nalle was often seen by one H. F. Averill, formerly connected with one of the papers of this city, who communicated with his reputed owner in Virginia, and gave the information that led to a knowledge of the whereabouts of the fugitive. Averill wrote letters for him, and thus obtained an acquaintance with his history. Mr. Hansborough sent on an agent, Henry J. Wall, by whom the necessary papers were got out to arrest the fugitive.

Yesterday morning about 11 o'clock, Charles Nalle was sent to procure some bread for the family by whom he was employed. He failed to return. At the baker's, he was arrested by Deputy United States Marshal J. W. Holmes, and immediately taken before United States Commissioner Miles Beach. The son of Mr. Gilbert, thinking it strange that he did not come back, sent to the house of William Henry, on Division Street, where he boarded, and his whereabouts was discovered.

The examination before Commissioner Beach was quite brief. The evidence of Averill and the agent was taken, and the Commissioner decided to remand Nalle to Virginia. The necessary papers were made out and given to the Marshal.

By this time it was two o'clock, and the fact began to be noised abroad that there was a fugitive slave in Mr. Beach's office, corner of State and First Streets. People in knots of ten or twelv collected near the entrance, looking at Nalle, who could be seen at an upper window. William Henry, a colored man, with whom Nalle boarded, commenced talking from the curb-stone in a loud voice to the crowd. He uttered such sentences as, "There is a fugitive slave in that office—pretty soon you will see him come forth. He is going to be taken down South, and you will have a chance to see him. He is to be taken to the depot, to go to Virginia in the first train. Keep watch of those stairs, and you will have a sight." A number of women kept shouting, crying, and by loud appeals excited the colored persons assembled.

Still the crowd grew in numbers. Wagons halted in front of the locality, and were soon piled with spectators. An alarm of fire was sounded, and hose carriages dashed through the ranks of men, women, and boys; but they closed again, and kept looking with expectant eyes at the window where the negro was visible. Meanwhile, angry discussions commenced. Some persons agitated a rescue, and others favored law and order. Mr. Brockway, a lawyer, had his coat torn for expressing his sentiments; and other melees kept the interest alive.

All at once there was a wild hulloa, and every

eye was turned up to see the legs and part of the body of the prisoner protruding from the second-story window, at which he was endeavoring to escape. Then arose a shout! "Drop him!" "Catch him!" "Hurrah!" But the attempt was a fruitless one, for somebody in the office pulled Nalle back again, amid the shouts of a hundred pair of lungs. The crowd at this time numbered nearly a thousand persons. Many of them were black, and a good share were of the female sex. They blocked up State Street from First Street to the alley, and kept surging to and fro.

Martin I. Townsend, Esq., who acted as counsel for the fugitive, did not arrive in the Commissioner's office until a decision had been rendered. He immediately went before Judge Gould, of the Supreme Court, and procured a writ of habeas corpus in the usual form, *returnable* immediately. This was given Deputy Sheriff Nathaniel Upham, who at once proceeded to Commissioner Beach's office, and served it on Holmes. Very injudiciously, the officers proceeded at once to Judge Gould's office, although it was evident they would have to pass through an excited, unreasonable crowd. As soon as the officers and their prisoner emerged from the door, an old negro, who had been standing at the bottom of the stairs, shouted, "Here they come," and the crowd made a terrific rush at the party.

From the office of Commissioner Beach, in the Mutual Building, to that of Judge Gould, in Congress Street, is less than two blocks, but it was made a regular battle field. The moment the prisoner emerged from the doorway, in custody of Deputy-Sheriff Upham, Chief of Police Quin, Officers Cleveland and Holmes, the crowd made one grand charge, and those nearest the prisoner seized him violently, with the intention of pulling him away from the officers, but they were foiled; and down First to Congress Street, and up the latter in front of Judge Gould's chambers, went the surging mass. Exactly what did go on in the crowd, it is impossible to say, but the pulling, hauling, mauling, and shouting, gave evidences of frantic efforts on the part of the rescuers, and a stern resistance from the conservators of the law. In front of Judge Gould's office the combat was at its height. No stones or other missiles were used; the battle was fist to fist. We believe an order was given to take the prisoner the other way, and there was a grand rush towards the West, past First and River Streets, as far as Dock Street. All this time there was a continual melee. Many of the officers were hurt—

among them Mr. Upham, whose object was solely to do his duty by taking Nalle before Judge Gould in accordance with the writ of habeas corpus. A number in the crowd were more or less hurt, and it is a wonder that these were not badly injured, as pistols were drawn and chisels used.

The battle had raged as far as the corner of Dock and Congress Streets, and the victory remained with the rescuers at last. The officers were completely worn out with their exertions, and it was impossible to continue their hold upon him any longer. Nalle was at liberty. His friends rushed him down Dock Street to the lower ferry, where there was a skiff lying ready to start. The fugitive was put in, the ferryman rowed off, and amid the shouts of hundreds who lined the banks of the river, Nalle was carried into Albany County.

As the skiff landed in West Troy, a negro sympathizer waded up to the waist, and pulled Nalle out of the boat. He went up the hill alone, however, and there who should he meet but Constable Becker? The latter official seeing a man with manacles on, considered it his duty to arrest him. He did so, and took him in a wagon to the office of Justice Stewart, on the second floor of the corner building near the ferry. The Justice was absent.

When the crowd on the Troy bank had seen Nalle safely landed, it was suggested that he might be recaptured. Then there was another rush made for the steam ferry-boat, which carried over about 400 persons, and left as many more—a few of the latter being soused in their efforts to get on the boat. On landing in West Troy, there, sure enough, was the prisoner, locked up in a strong office, protected by Officers Becker, Brown and Morrison, and the door barricaded.

Not a moment was lost. Up stairs went a score or more of resolute men—the rest "piling in" promiscuously, shouting and execrating the officers. Soon a stone flew against the door—then another—and bang, bang! went off a couple of pistols, but the officers who fired them took good care to aim pretty high. The assailants were forced to retreat for a moment. "They 've got pistols," said one. "Who cares?" was the reply; "they can only kill a dozen of us—come on." More stones and more pistol-shots ensued. At last the door was pulled open by an immense negro, and in a moment he was felled by a hatchet in the hands of Deputy-Sheriff Morrison; but the body of the fallen man blocked up the door so that it could not be shut, and a friend of the prisoner pulled him out. Poor fellow! he might well say, "Save me from my friends." Amid the pulling and hauling, the iron had cut his arms, which were bleeding profusely, and he could hardly walk, owing to fatigue.

He has since arrived safely in Canada.

Statements made by Martin I. Townsend, Esq., of Troy, who was counsel for the fugitive, Charles Nalle.

Nalle is an octoroon; his wife has the same infusion of Caucasian blood. She was the daughter of her master, and had, with her sister, been bred by him in his family, as his own child. When the father died, both of these daughters were married and had large families of children. Under the highly Christian national laws of "Old Virginny," these children were the slaves of their grandfather. The old man died, leaving a will, whereby he manumitted his daughters and their children, and provided for the purchase of the freedom of their husbands. The manumission of the children and grandchildren took effect; but the estate was insufficient to purchase the husbands of his daughters, and the father of his grandchildren. The manumitted, by another Christian, "conservative," and "national" provision of law, were forced to leave the State, while the slave husbands remained in slavery. Nalle and his brother-in-law were allowed for a while to visit their families outside Virginia about once a year, but were at length ordered to provide themselves with new wives, as they would be allowed to visit their former ones no more. It was after this that Nalle and his brother-in-law started for the land of freedom, guided by the steady light of the north star. Thank God, neither family now need fear any earthly master or the bay of the blood-hound dogging their fugitive steps.

Nalle returned to Troy with his family about July, 1860, and resided with them there for more than seven years. They are all now residents of the city of Washington, D. C. Nalle and his family are persons of refined manners, and of the highest respectability. Several of his children are red-haired, and a stranger would discover no trace of African blood in their complexions or features. It was the head of this family whom H. F. Averill proposed to doom to returnless exile and life-long slavery.

When Nalle was brought from Commissioner Beach's office into the street, Harriet Tubman, who had been standing with the excited crowd, rushed amongst the foremost to Nalle, and running one of her arms around his manacled arm, held on to him without ever loosening her hold through the more than half-hour's struggle to Judge Gould's office, and from Judge Gould's office to the dock, where Nalle's liberation was accomplished. In the melee, she was repeatedly beaten over the head with policemen's clubs, but she never for a moment released her hold, but cheered Nalle and his friends with her voice, and struggled with the officers until they were literally worn out with their exertions, and Nalle was separated from them.

True, she had strong and earnest helpers in her struggle, some of whom had white faces as well as human hearts, and are now in Heaven. But she exposed herself to the fury of the sympathizers with slavery, without fear, and suffered their blows without flinching. Harriet crossed the river with the crowd, in the ferry-boat, and when the men who led the assault upon the door of Judge Stewart's office, were stricken down, Harriet and a number of other colored women rushed over their bodies, brought Nalle out, and putting him in the first wagon passing, started him for the West.

A livery team, driven by a colored man, was immediately sent on to relieve the other, and Nalle was seen about Troy no more until he returned a free man by purchase from his master. Harriet also disappeared, and the crowd dispersed. How she came to be in Troy that day, is entirely unknown to our citizens; and where she hid herself after the rescue, is equally a mystery. But her struggle was in the sight of a thousand, perhaps of five thousand spectators.

This woman of whom you have been reading is poor, and partially disabled from her injuries; yet she supports cheerfully and uncomplainingly herself and her old parents, and always has several poor children in her house, who are dependent entirely upon her exertions. At present she has three of these children for whom she is providing, while their parents are working to pay back money borrowed to bring them on. She also maintains by her exertions among the good people of Auburn, two schools of freedmen at the South, providing them teachers and sending them clothes and books. She never asks for anything for herself, but she does ask the charity of the public for "her people."

For them her tears will fall,
For them her prayers ascend;
To them her toils and cares be given,
Till toils and cares will end.

If any persons are disposed to aid her in her benevolent efforts, they may send donations to Rev. S. M. Hopkins, Professor in the Auburn Theological Seminary, who will make such disposition of the funds sent as may be designated by the donors.

APPENDIX.

APPENDIX.

A few circumstances having come out in conversation with Harriet, they are added here, as they may be of interest to the reader.

On asking Harriet particularly as to the age of her mother, she answered, "Well, I'll tell you, Missis. Twenty-three years ago, in Maryland, I paid a lawyer $5 to look up the will of my mother's first master. He looked back sixty years, and said it was time to give up. I told him to go back furder. He went back sixty-five years, and there he found the will—giving the girl Ritty to his grand-daughter (Mary Patterson), to serve her and her offspring till she was forty-five years of age. This grand-daughter died soon after, unmarried; and as there was no provision for Ritty, in case of her death, she was actually emancipated at that time. But no one informed her of the fact, and she and her dear children remained in bondage till emancipated by the courage and determination of this heroic daughter and sister. The old woman must then, it seems, be ninety-eight years of age, and the old man has probably numbered as many years. And yet these old people, living out beyond the toll-gate, on the South Street road, Auburn, come in every Sunday—more than a mile—to the Central Church. To be sure, deep slumbers settle down upon them as soon as they are seated, which continue undisturbed till the congregation is dismissed; but they have done their best, and who can doubt that they receive a blessing. Immediately after this they go to class-meeting at the Methodist Church. Then they wait for a third service, and after that start out home again.

On asking Harriet where they got anything to eat on Sunday, she said, in her quiet way, "Oh! de ole folks nebber eats anyting on *Sunday*, Missis! We nebber has no food to get for dem on Sunday. Dey always fasts; and dey nebber eats anyting on Fridays. Good Friday, an' five Fridays hand gwine from Good Friday, my fader nebber eats or drinks, all day—fasting for de five bleeding wounds ob Jesus. All the oder Fridays ob de year he nebber eats till de sun goes down; den he takes a little tea an' a piece ob bread." "But is he a Roman Catholic, Harriet?" "Oh no, Misses; he does it for *conscience;* we was taught to do so down South. He says if he denies himself for the sufferings of his Lord an' Master, Jesus will sustain him."

It has been mentioned that Harriet never asks anything for herself, but whenever her people were in trouble, or she felt impelled to go South to guide to freedom friend or brother, or father and mother, if she had not time to work for the money, she was persistent till she got it from somebody. When she received one of her *intimations* that the old people were in trouble, and it was time for her to go to them, she asked the Lord where she should go for the money. She was in some way, as she supposed, directed to the office of a certain gentleman in New York. When she left the house of her friends to go there, she said, "I'm gwine to Mr. ——'s office, an' I ain't gwine to lebe there, an' I ain't gwine to eat or drink till I git enough money to take me down after the ole people."

She went into this gentleman's office.

"What do you want, Harriet?" was the first greeting.

"I want some money, sir."

"You do? How much do you want?"

"I want twenty dollars, sir."

"*Twenty dollars?* Who told you to come here for twenty dollars?"

"De Lord tole me, sir."

"Well, I guess the Lord's mistaken this time."

"I guess he isn't, sir. Anyhow I'm gwine to sit here till I git it."

So she sat down and went to sleep. All the morning and all the afternoon she sat there still, sleeping and rousing up—sometimes finding the office full of gentlemen—sometimes finding herself alone. Many fugitives were passing through New York at that time, and those who came in supposed that she was one of them, tired out and resting. Sometimes she would be roused up with the words, "Come, Harriet, you had better go. There's no money for you here." "No, sir. I'm not gwine till I git my twenty dollars."

She does not know all that happened, for deep sleep fell upon her; but probably her story was whispered about, and she roused at last to find herself the happy possessor of *sixty dollars*, which had been raised among those who came into the office. She went on her way rejoicing, to bring her old parents from the land of bondage. She found that her father was to be tried the next Monday, for helping off slaves; so, as she says, she "removed his trial to a higher court," and hurried him off to Canada. One more little incident, which, it is hoped, may not be offensive to the young lady to whom it alludes, may be mentioned here, showing Harriet's extreme delicacy in asking anything for herself. Last winter ('67 and '68), as we all know, the snow was very deep for months, and Harriet and the old people were completely snowed-in in their little home. The old man was laid up with rheumatism, and Harriet could not leave home for a long time to procure supplies of corn, if she could have made her way into the city. At length, stern necessity compelled her to plunge through the drifts to the city, and she appeared at the house of one of her firm and fast friends, and was directed to the room of one of the young ladies. She began to walk up and down, as she always does when in trouble. At length she said, "Miss Annie?" "What, Harriet?" A long pause; then again, "Miss Annie?" "Well, what *is* it, Harriet?" This was repeated four times, when the young lady, looking up, saw her eyes filled with tears. She then insisted on knowing what she wanted. And with a great effort, she said, "Miss Annie, could you lend me a quarter till Monday? I never asked it before." Kind friends immediately supplied all the wants of the family, but on Monday Harriet appeared with the quarter she had borrowed.

But though so timid for herself, she is bold enough when the wants of her race are concerned. Even now, while friends are trying to raise the means to publish this little book for her, *she* is going around with the greatest zeal and interest to raise a subscription for her Freedmen's Fair. She called on Hon. Wm. H. Seward, the other day, for a subscription to this object. He said, "Harriet, you have worked for others long enough. It is time you should think of yourself. If you ask for a donation for *yourself*, I will give it to you; but I will not help you to rob yourself for others."

Harriet's charity for all the human race is unbounded. It embraces even the slaveholder—it sympathizes even with Jeff. Davis, and rejoices at his departure to other lands, with some prospect of peace for the future. She says, "I tink dar's many a slaveholder 'll git to Heaven. Dey don't know no better. Dey acts up to de light dey hab. You take dat sweet little child (pointing to a lonely baby)—'pears more like an angel dan any-ting else—take her down dere, let her nebber know nothing 'bout niggers but they was made to be whipped, an' she 'll grow up to use the whip on 'em jus' like de rest. No, Missus, its because dey don't know no better." May God give the people to whom the story of this woman shall come, a like charity, so that through their kindness the last days of her stormy and troubled life may be calm and peaceful.

ESSAY ON WOMAN-WHIPPING.

THE subject of the preceding memoir appears to have retained all her life a feeling recollection of the effects of the whip in the hands of her youthful mistress. Considering the vigor and frequency of the application, this is not strange. Infinite cuffs and thwacks, more or less, pass into oblivion; but a flogging with a raw-hide is not easily forgotten. A slave's experience of the whip, however, was not confined to his or to *her* early days. A slave race must be controlled by fear and pain; and the discipline, it was naturally thought, could not begin too early. From childhood to old age they were liable to stripes, for any reason or for no reason. If the slave was guilty of no fault, he might be whipped, as appears from the preceding narrative, merely to impress him with a salutary sense of the master's right and disposition to whip.

A Northern man, born and bred under the influences of freedom and the protection of law, and made acquainted with slavery in its old palmy days, can never forget his sensations at his first sight of a slave-whipping. The utmost he has ever seen in the way of corporal punishment has been the switching of some obstreperous child by competent authority; a discipline administered with prudence and moderation; drawing no blood and leaving no scar. He now sees an adult person stripped to the skin, his arms tied at their utmost stretch above his head, or across some object which binds him into a posture the best adapted to feel the full force of each blow. The instrument of suffering is not a birch twig or a ferule, but a twisted raw-hide, or heavy "black snake;" either of them highly effective weapons in the hands of a stout executioner. Our Northern novice stands horror-stricken and paralyzed for a moment; but at the second or third blow, and the piteous scream of *Oh Lord! Massa!* which follows, he digs his fingers into his ears, and rushes to the furthest corner of his tent or dwelling, to escape the scene. Even if he *could* have endured the sight and sound a while longer, he dared not. The horror in his face, and perhaps the irrepressible word or act of interference was too sure to bring upon himself the vengeance due to a "d—d Abolitionist." The little knot of Southern *habitués* look on with critical inspection, squirting tobacco-juice, with their hands in their pockets.

If the subject is a woman, the interest rises higher, and the crowd would be greater. There is a refinement of cruelty in the whipping of a woman which used to stimulate agreeably the dull sensibilities of a Southern mob. A dish of torture had to be peppered very high to please the palates of those epicures in brutality. The helplessness and terror of the victim, the exposure of her person, the opportunity for coarse jests at her expense, all combined to make it a scene of rare enjoyment. How the "chivalric" mind can endure the loss of such gratifications it is difficult to conceive. The Romans were weaned from crucifixions and gladiatorial combats very gradually. The process of ameliorating criminal law and humanizing public sentiment went on for more than two centuries. It was full four hundred years after the epoch of our redemption when the monk Telemachus threw himself between the hired swordsmen, whom a Christian audience was applauding, and laid down his own life to wind up the spectacle. But the bloody morsel has been snatched from the mouths of the "chivalry" at one clutch. No wonder their mortification vents itself in weeping and wailing, and knashing of teeth, and in such miscellaneous atrocities as their "Ku-Klux-Klans" can venture to inflict on helpless freedmen and radicals.*

A recent Southern paper (the *Virginia Advertiser*) finds a providential provision for the enslavement of the negro race in the thickness of their skulls, enabling them to bear without injury the blows inflicted in sudden rage by their masters; a suggestive confession, by the way, of the influence of slavery on the tempers of the slaveholders. The whole race must be prepared, it seems, for blows on the head with whatever weapon came to hand! But admitting the thickness of the skulls, it appears from an incident in the preceding pages, as well as from other known instances, that the inventive genius of the slave-whipping chivalry contrived to baffle the humane designs of Providence—a negro skull well padded with wool might bear without injury the blow of a boot-jack or a hammer, and yet prove insufficient to resist the impact of a musket-ball or a ten-pound weight.

* It is curiously illustrative of the mixed childishness and ferocity which characterizes the Southern civilization, that this secret association of ruffians, organized to terrorize the loyal South, styles itself by an absurd, mis-spelled name, and goes about on its nightly work of murder in harlequin costume, with one of its leaders acting the part of ghost, to frighten the superstitious blacks. Some more courageous freedman occasionally makes a *bona fide* ghost of this masquerade.

It is of no avail to plate a vessel with six inches of iron, if she is to be pounded with bolts that can mash an eight-inch armor. Apparently, Divine Providence stopped short of the necessary security for the predestined slave race. It should have arranged for a progressive thickening of the negro cranium to meet the increase of violence on the part of the master; until at length slavery might be encountered with a difficulty like that which besets naval gunnery, viz., what would be the result if an infrangible African skull should be beaten by an irresistable Caucasian club?

But even this Virginia *laudator temporis acti*, this melancholy mourner at the tomb of defunct slavery, does not allege any such Providential thickening of the negro cuticle as to amount to a satisfactory anæsthesis against whipping. It has never been proven that a Virginia paddle or a Georgia raw-hide well applied did not make the blood spirt as freely through a black skin as through a white one; nor has any Southern savant of the Nott and Gliddon school shown that there was not the same *relative* delicacy of organization in the slave woman as in the free. A black woman was, relatively to the black man, the more delicate subject for the whip; something more sensitive to the shame of stripping, more liable to terror, and of rather softer fiber; so that the lash went deeper both into soul and sense than in the case of her sable brother.

And this fact made the black woman a very suitable subject for the whip in the hands of the Southern lady. To succeed in slave-whipping as in any other fine art, the Horatian canon must be regarded, which requires us to take a subject suited to our strength. It would have been unreasonable, in ordinary cases, to expect a "dark-eyed daughter of the South" to flog handsomely a stalwart negro man; she sometimes did it, after he had been well tied up. But the slave girl was exactly suited to her flagellating capacities. A good many women, North as well as South, manifest a tendency to become tyrants in their own households, and love to bully their servants. But this is an evil of a mitigated nature in Northern society. The stupidest "help" in the kitchen knows she is safe from any other lash than her mistress' tongue, and is commonly an adept at the business of answering back again.

But the Southern mistress was a domestic devil with horns and claws; selfish, insolent, accustomed to be waited on for everything. She grew up with the instinct of tyranny—to punish violently the leâst neglect or disobedience in her servants. The variable temper of girlhood, not ugly unless thwarted, became in the "Southern matron" a chronic fury. She was her own "overseer," and, like that out-door functionary, had her own scepter, which she did not bear in vain. The raw-hide lay upon the shelf within easy reach, and her arm was vigorous with exercise. The breaking of a plate, the spilling of a cup, the misplacing of a pin in her dress, or any other misadventure in the chapter of accidents, was promptly illustrated with numerous cuts. The lash well laid on the shoulders of a black *femme-de-chambre*, or screaming child, was an agreeable titillation of the nervous sensibilities of the languid creole; a headache, or a heartache, transferred itself through the medium of the raw-hide to the back of Phillis or Araminta. They no doubt whipped sometimes, like Mr. Squeers, for the mere fun of the thing. It is an exquisite pleasure to a cowardly nature to have some creature to torment; and there is this nemesis about cruelty that it engenders an appetite which, like that for alcoholic stimulents, for ever demands increased indulgence. It was the vindictive woman's nature in the South that protracted and gave added ferocity to the rebellion. These woman-whipping wives and mothers it was who hounded on the masculine chivalry to the work of exterminating the "accursed Yankees," and thus made their own punishment so much sorer than it need have been.

The mention of these amiable Southern characteristics cannot fail to recall that highly suggestive scene of the Malebolge, with the illustration of Gustave Doré, in which the tempters and destroyers of women are seen scourged with whips, in the hands of demons; especially when we remember that the whipping of slave women to make them consent to their own dishonor, was one of the usages of the patriarchal chivalry. There is not a scene in which the imaginings of Dante have been better seconded by the pencil of the great French artist: the flying wretches hurrying in opposite directions, as the crowds in the Jubilee year trampled each other, going and returning across the St. Angelo Bridge; among them the bat-winged fiends with whips, lashing right and left! In the throng are female figures: women who in life tortured and corrupted other women. What terror in face an attitude! How desperately they grapple with the rocks to lift themselves out of reach of the scourge! And these two demons in the foreground! What an absolute idealization of muscular ferocity! Every sinewy line in their cantour displays the force of a fallen demi-god; their very tails curl with delight in their ministry of vengeance.

> Ahi; come facen lèvar le berze,
> Alle prime percosse, e gia nessuno,
> Le second aspettava ne le terze!

Ah! how they make them skip! There is Legree and Tom Gordon, and Madame de Schlangenbad, from Louisiana, and Mrs. Crawley (*neé* Sharp) from South Carolina, squirming under the torture! A very instructive, if not agreeable exhibition!

But this fury in celestial Southern bosoms was merely institutional. Dip the gentlest nature into the element of irresponsible power, and it becomes in time covered over with a foul incrustation of cruelty. Those beastly Roman ladies of Juvenal's time, who could order a slave woman to be whipped to death without condescending to give any other reason than their *sic volo, sic jubeo*, were not naturally worse than others. Take any Roman or Southern girl of ten years of age, put a whip in her hands, and a helpless slave child at her mercy; let her see nothing but brutality to inferiors all around her, and by the time she is ready to be married, she can hold up her thumb to the standing gladiator in the arena, or beg her lover to bring her back from Bull Run a ring from the bones of some Yan kee soldier. It is a publicly known private fact, illustrative of the influence of slavery on the female character, that when a certain Northern clergyman applied to her father for the hand of a celebrated Maryland heiress, the reply was, "You are quite welcome to her! but I think it only fair to tell you that if I were going to storm hell, I should put her in the advance."

There is every reason to hope, therefore, that the Southern character, both male and female, will become gradually ameliorated by the changed condition under which it will hereafter be formed. It is a common error, one in which the Southern people themselves share, that there is something in their climate to nurse and to justify their "high spirit," *anglicé* their quarrelsomeness and brutality of temper. It is very pleasant to lay off upon Nature or Providence what belongs only to will or institutions. A man indulges in violent passions with little restraint or remorse, so long as he can persuade himself he is merely what certain positive natural laws make him. What an opiate for a conscience defiled with lust and blood, to think that this is only natural to the "sunny South." But in fact, the people of warm, temperate, and tropical regions are most commonly gentle of mood; the climate acts as an anodyne, and soothes them into a peaceful equilibrium of the passions. The negroes of the Southern States are not passionate or vindictive—well for their late masters and present persecutors that they are not! What they may become from the treatment they are experiencing from those preternatural and predestinated fools, is another question.

The only reason the "chivalry" are bad-tempered and quarrelsome, is found in that despotism in which they have been nursed, and which associates the idea of personal dignity with an instant resort to violence at any contradiction. But for slavery, the people of Mississippi would have been no more addicted to street fights, dueling, midnight assassinations, etc., than the people of Massachusetts. That the former have any advantage in respect to courage, has been sufficiently disproved by the rebellion. Whether the ex-Confederate ladies may or may not be able to "fire the Southern heart" for another attempt to overthrow the Government, it will at least never be done under the persuasion that one Southerner is equal to five or any other number above unity, of Yankees.

The traditions of slavery, indeed, will remain to

keep alive among the late slaveholding caste, the insolent and unchristian temper on which they have prided themselves. But having no more helpless dependants to storm at and abuse, their valor will needs submit to gradual modifications. Some degree of self-government will become a necessity. It may require several generations; but *institutions* ceasing to corrupt them, the loss of wealth, the necessity of work and a new Gospel of peace, better than their old slaveholding Christianity, will gradually educate them into a law-abiding, orderly, and virtuous people.

The Southern woman will of course share early in this beneficent change—no longer perverted into a she-devil by the possession of unrestrained power, and paying just wages to servants, who, if not suited with their work, can leave without having to run off; her gentler virtues will have a chance to assert themselves. Her striking qualities will subside into a charming vivacity of temper. She will become a gracious and pious mater-familias; she will perhaps in time learn to apply to her own children a portion of that discipline of which her slaves enjoyed a monopoly. In short, there neither is nor ever was any reason, slavery excepted, why the Southern whites should not possess a character for industry, peacefulness, and religion, equal to that of the rural districts of New York and New England.

Thank God that we have lived to see such awful barbarisms extinct! In fifty years the last woman-whipper at the South will be as dead as Cleopatra; as dead as the pre-Adamite brute organizations. History will be ashamed to record their doings. The fictions in which they are enbalmed will be lost in the better coming era of morals and letters. By the time the South has been overflowed and regenerated by a beneficent inundation of Northern "carpet-baggers," with Yankee capital and enterprise, it will be forgotten that a race capable of the crimes referred to in the preceding story, ever existed.

CPSIA information can be obtained
at www.ICGtesting.com
Printed in the USA
LVOW11s0108021216
515442LV00001B/19/P